HISTORIC HOUSES III

San Juan Neighborhood
Stanford University

STANFORD HISTORICAL SOCIETY

Stanford, California

Stanford Historical Society
P.O. Box 20028
Stanford, CA 94309
(650) 725-3332
http://histsoc.stanford.edu

COVER

Ageless California valley oak in the center of El Escarpado Way
is focal point for the late-1920s Tudor-style houses on the cul-de-sac.

PAINTING – BYRON FEIG

10 9 8 7 6 5 4 3 2 1

Printed on acid-free paper
in the United States of America
Bembo font (body text 10 pt. on 14 pt. leading)

ISBN: 0-9664249-4-8

TABLE OF CONTENTS

ACKNOWLEDGMENTS

Many volunteers have contributed to this volume, and the Stanford Historical Society thanks them all.

RESEARCH AND WRITING

Marian Leib Adams
Dick Bennett
Kathy Cusick
Therese Baker-Degler
Hill Gates
John Harbaugh
Grace Hinton
Ann Kay
Philip D. Leighton
Mandy MacCalla
Virginia Mann
Sophia McConnell
Debby Robbins
DeeDee Schurman
Susan Sweeney
David and Natalie Weber
Phyllis and Robert White

EDITING AND FACT-CHECKING

Marian Leib Adams
Karen Bartholomew
Julie Cain
Lyn Carr
Margaret McKinnon
Roxanne Nilan

PHOTOGRAPHY

Leni Hazlett
Margaret McKinnon

ARCHIVAL ASSISTANCE AND RESEARCH

Margaret Kimball
Miriam Palm
Steve Staiger

STANFORD'S OFFICES OF FACULTY HOUSING, MAPS AND RECORDS, AND PLANNING

Elena Angoloti
Cindy Kirby
Betty Oen
Jan Thomson
Ruth Todd

Executive editor/production editor: **Karen Bartholomew**
Editor: **Margaret Learmonth McKinnon**
Director of research and writing: **Marian Leib Adams**
Historical consultant: **Roxanne Nilan, Ph.D.**
Designer: **Joanna McClean,** MacWorks Graphics Studio
Chief photographer: **Leni Hazlett**
Illustrator: **Byron A. Feig, '05**
Printer: **Shoreline Printing & Graphics, Inc.**

HOMEOWNERS WHO SHARED THEIR HOMES, HOUSE PLANS, AND MEMORIES

Jim and Marian Adams
Joe Bankman and Barbara Fried
Dick Bennett and Ann Kay
Paul and Christina Cohen
Bill and Pat Dement
Helen Mears Gibson
Paul Goldstein and Jan Thompson
Trevor and Lynda Hastie
The Guerard family
Hallie Spurr Heckler and Herb Heckler
Harden and Sophia McConnell
Robert and Debby Robbins
David and DeeDee Schurman
Sheila and Laurie Spaeth
Judith Swain and Edward Holmes
James and Susan Sweeney
Robert and Phyllis White
Arthur Wolf and Hill Gates

❋ ❋ ❋

We hope that these efforts will inspire further research on Stanford's historic houses, and an appreciation of Stanford's history and architectural heritage.

Marian Leib Adams, Co-Chair
Historic Houses Committee
May 2005

INTRODUCTION

Old houses tell wonderful stories, and the histories of the early faculty homes at Stanford tell of the beginnings of a great university through the professors and families of those early years.

This book, the latest in a series about campus houses built before 1930, includes reports on 17 houses in what is generally known as the San Juan subdivision, district, or neighborhood (see map inside the front cover).

Today's San Juan neighborhood includes the residential area bounded by Alvarado Row on the northeast, Campus Drive to the northwest, Junipero Serra Boulevard to the southwest, and Frenchman's Road and Coronado Avenue on the east. The area also includes student residences, thus keeping alive the Stanfords' wish for a residential campus with faculty and students as neighbors.

The first house on San Juan Hill was built in 1900 by George B. and Linda Cooksey, friends of the Stanfords, as a winter home. It looked down at the main residential streets of Alvarado and Salvatierra. The neighborhood started growing in earnest in 1905, when Harris J. Ryan built his house at 9 (now 607) Cabrillo Street and William F. Durand built at 11 (now 623) Cabrillo.

In the early days, street names and numbers changed, but by 1930 most of them were set. The oldest houses in this book, built on a stretch of road on the north side of the reservoir at the apex of San Juan Hill, had three different addresses. From 1907 to 1910, the road was called Aibonito, but President David Starr Jordan considered the name unappealing and after 1910 renamed it Cabrillo. Between 1924 and 1928, it took on the name Santa Ynez Street, as an extension of the road that ran up from Alvarado Row (maps and telephone directories give conflicting names for those four years).

In the 1920s, the university, needing more faculty housing, pushed into a new area, known as San Juan Subdivision No. 3. It included lots along Gerona Road, Santa Maria Avenue, and El Escarpado Way.

All the houses featured here can be described as eclectic period style, which was dominant from the late 19th century up to about 1940. This movement borrowed from many architectural traditions. The five earliest houses, built before World War I, range from Craftsman and Italian Renaissance to California cottage and adobe, with two Tudors in the mix. More than half of the houses described here are in predominantly Tudor style and were built in the late 1920s. Spanish eclectic, English cottage, and French country also appear. The dominance of the Tudor style shows off spectacularly in the four houses on El Escarpado Way, off Gerona Road near Campus Drive. Three are by Charles Sumner, the fourth by Binder and Curtis; see the introduction to this street on page 14.

The houses in this book highlight the careers of several prominent Bay Area architects and builders of the early 20th century, in particular John Kennedy Branner, son of geology professor and Stanford's second president, John Casper Branner; Birge Clark, a Stanford graduate and son of art professor and architect Arthur Bridgeman Clark; and Charles Kaiser Sumner, who designed more than 30 campus houses, including seven (perhaps eight) of the houses in this book. Branner and Clark each designed two houses, and John Bakewell Jr. of Bakewell and Brown of San Francisco, Binder and Curtis of San Jose, A. W. Smith of Oakland, and Walter H. Ratcliff Jr. of Berkeley each designed one. Designer-contractor George Wilbert Mosher also designed and built one house.

Separate biographies of Branner, Clark, and Sumner begin on page 6.

We hope that those who read these accounts—researched over the past several years by numerous volunteers for the Stanford Historical Society—will enjoy them and develop an appreciation for Stanford's rich heritage of residential architecture.

—Marian Leib Adams

The ARCHITECTS

~ John K. Branner

John Kennedy Branner, who designed more than a dozen houses on the Stanford campus, was the elder son of Susan Kennedy Branner and John Casper Branner—head of Stanford's Geology Department beginning in 1892 and second president of the university (1913–15). The younger Branner, born in Arkansas in 1886, grew up on campus in the family home on Alvarado Row.

From 1905 to 1908, he studied geology at Stanford, then left to study architecture at Columbia University, graduating in 1912. He traveled and studied in Europe, and spent some time in New York. He never married, and when he returned to California he made his home with his mother on Alvarado Row. (The Branner house, next door to the Griffin-Drell house, at Alvarado Row and Campus Drive, was torn down for a parking lot in the 1970s.)

Branner was a practicing architect for 46 years, with an office in San Francisco, at 519 California Street, and later at 251 Kearny Street. He was living in San Francisco when he died, in 1968.

Specializing in residences, Branner designed 14 houses on campus between 1909 and 1936. Their designs accommodated his clients' desires and specifications, creating an eclectic collection of styles. Several of his campus houses are brown-shingle structures, often classified as California Craftsman or First Bay Tradition. He also worked in the Mediterranean style, popular at the time. Some of his homes are similar to those designed by Birge Clark, another respected Palo Alto and campus architect, who was known for his Spanish period style structures.

The house at 766 Santa Ynez, designed and built for Professor Clelia Mosher in 1926, reflects a Mediterranean style she had come to know while in

John K. Branner, second from right, with his parents and siblings in a photo taken about 1920 that mimicked one taken when the children were youngsters. Flanking John are Elsie, two years his senior, and George, five years his junior. In 1896 and '97, the children entertained the campus with their pamphlet-type newspaper, Little Nonsense.

Europe. The French country house at 635 Gerona, which he designed in 1927 for Professor and Mrs. Albert L. Guérard, is reminiscent of houses in Guérard's native France. Some of his other structures include the 1915 Tudor period style house at 755 Santa Ynez, built for classics Professor Henry R. Fairclough, the 1926 Wolter house at 692 Mirada, and the 1935 Sellards house at 716 Salvatierra (see page 8). The Guérard and Fairclough houses are described in this book.

Branner was also hired to design houses for campus fraternities and sororities. His 1917 design for the Zeta Psi house (today's Bechtel International Center, across from the Faculty Club), reflects a European style and was a fitting assignment for one who had been a member of the Stanford chapter. In the 1930s, his remodel of the original shingle-style Kappa Alpha Theta house into a largely colonial revival structure (now Columbae House, 549 Lasuen Mall) received an honor award from the Northern California chapter of the American Institute of Architects.

Passionate about Stanford architecture, Branner pleaded with the Board of Trustees in 1913 to hire a distinguished architect to design the new Main Library. A portion of his letter to Timothy Hopkins reveals his feelings about Stanford's place in architectural history:

> I can well remember when Stanford's only boast was the beautiful inner quadrangle surrounded by poppy fields, and I deeply regret that since the days of the old quad, architectural matters have been so neglected. The inner quadrangle remains to-day as the most beautiful and inspiring thing on campus, but it was designed by a firm of architects [Shepley, Rutan and Coolidge] who in their day were the masters of their profession....
>
> I feel that during your regime as president of the Board of Trustees, the greatest possible service which can be rendered Stanford would be a return to Senator Stanford's wise stand and long ago forgotten policy of employing the best possible architects for her buildings, as it is through them, that unnumbered generations to come, must judge the present.

Branner also was involved with the design of public buildings at Stanford. In 1915, he designed a popular change in the façade of Memorial Church. In the wake of the 1906 earthquake, the Board of Trustees had decided to replace the façade's original giant dedication inscription, but when the work was completed in 1914, the replacement was widely deemed an artistic failure. The swamplike scene of plants with calla lilies at the center produced the illusion that the windows were floating on plants. Branner's suggested design specified stone panels below the windows and the arches separating them, thus creating pillars for the bases of the arches and unifying the windows and arches with the ledge below. He called for simple mosaic designs between the stone pillars using leftover mosaics on hand. Trustees endorsed the plan in early 1915, and the façade was quickly and permanently changed.

In 1927, Branner designed an arcade-style superstructure of bleachers around the rim of the 1921 Stanford Stadium, gaining 16,500 seats for a total seating capacity of approximately 87,000. The arches of Branner's addition echo the arches of the Quadrangle.

When Branner died, he left his estate in trust for his sister, Elsie B. Fowler; she had access to the trust's income, but the principal was designated to UC Berkeley's School of

The Branner house was between the 10th house of the Alvarado Row "Decalogue" and the Griffin house. Barely visible on the porch, John stands next to his mother, Susan, who holds George. Mrs. Branner's mother is at left and daughter Elsie stands with bicycle at foot of stairs.

Architecture to endow one or more John K. Branner Traveling Fellowships for outstanding students. Holders of the prestigious fellowships go overseas to explore a particular architectural question or issue that may later be expanded as a thesis; France and Italy must be included in their itineraries. In 2004, four students received $25,000 each to spend nine months abroad.

—MANDY MACCALLA

A $10,000 house—designed by John K. Branner in 1935 and offered a decade later in the 1946 California Plan Book—was built for John Sellards at 716 Salvatierra. Edwin Coman was a later occupant.

SOURCES

Bacon, Rosamond, and Karen Bartholomew. "Branner Children Entertained Campus with Publishing Venture." *Sandstone & Tile* (Stanford Historical Society) 12, no. 1 (Fall 1987): 7–11.

Bartholomew, Karen, and Roxanne Nilan. "Rivalry and Entrepreneurship Mark 1921 Construction of Stanford Stadium." *Sandstone & Tile* (Stanford Historical Society) 9, no. 1 (Autumn 1984): 1-6.

Branner, John K., to Timothy Hopkins (15 November 1913). Board of Trustees Supporting Documents, Box 9, Folder 11, Stanford University Archives.

Branner Traveling Fellowship. Description provided by Tracy Farbstein of the College of Environmental Design, UC Berkeley. Endowment Record Sheet provided by Dan Estropia of the UC Berkeley Development Office.

Bridges, Marjorie. "637 Alvarado Row." *Historic Houses of Lower San Juan District.* Stanford Historical Society (1998).

California Plan Book, 2nd and Enlarged Edition: Preview for 1946. Home Book Publishers.

Newfield, Elsbeth. "766 Santa Ynez." *Historic Houses of San Juan Hill.* Stanford Historical Society (1995).

Pratt, Constance. "649 Mirada." *Historic Houses of San Juan Hill.* Stanford Historical Society (1995).

Stanford Alumnus 16, no. 6 (February 1915): 227; and no. 7 (March 1915): 272 [Memorial Church façade].

PHOTOS

Family photos, Stanford News Service; house plan, Palo Alto Historical Association.

~ Birge Clark

Birge Malcolm Clark, who was the product of Palo Alto and Stanford upbringing and education, designed many houses and public buildings in the town and on the campus, where he was well known and well loved.

Clark, born in San Francisco in 1893, was the son of Hanna Grace Birge and Arthur B. Clark, professor of art and architecture at Stanford and Mayfield's first mayor. Birge grew up in family homes at 2257 Hanover Street in College Terrace and 767 Santa Ynez (now 618 Mirada) on the campus, both of which his father had designed. After graduating from Palo Alto High School in 1910, he received his A.B. degree in graphic arts from Stanford in 1914, and a B.Arch. from Columbia University in 1917.

During World War I, Clark spent two years as an army officer and company commander in the balloon service in France, earning a Silver Star for gallantry in action. He was shot down once: he parachuted into the woods after a German pilot put eight bullet holes in his hydrogen-filled tethered balloon. Another time he was almost blown into enemy territory as his tangled observation balloon hovered at 3,000 feet.

Clark returned in 1919 and soon got his start on the Stanford campus as "clerk of the works," assisting his father and Lou Henry Hoover with the design of the house on San Juan Hill that now bears her name. Since 1945, it has been the residence of Stanford's president, and was designated a state historic landmark in 1978 and a national historic landmark in 1985.

After opening his first office in Palo Alto in 1922, Clark went on to design 39 campus houses, including several on San Juan Hill. He practiced on his own until 1928, then with his brother David until David's death, in 1944. Subsequently, he worked with partners Walter Stromquist, Joe Ehrlich, and David Potter; later partners were Paul Sandstrom, Jonathan Gifford, and Ernie Ericson.

During his career, Clark designed, or contributed to the design of, 450 buildings in the Palo Alto area, including more than 30 that are on the city's inventory of historic buildings and three that are on the National Register of Historic Places: the U.S. Post Office on Hamilton Avenue (1932); the Dunker house, 420 Maple Street; and the Charles and Kathleen Norris house, 1457 Cowper Street,

Three generations of Clarks in 1926: A. B. Clark is second from left in back row flanked by Birge and Esther, later a well-known pediatrician; also in the back row are twins David and Donald. Hanna Grace and Lucile Clark are in front with Birge and Lucile's children.

Birge Clark graduated from Stanford in 1914, then served in France during World War I.

which for several decades served as Stanford's Newman Center but is once again a private residence.

Others of Clark's landmark buildings in Palo Alto include the Lucie Stern Community Center (1935) and the old fire and police station, now Avenidas senior center, on Bryant Street. With artist/architect Pedro de Lemos, he designed the group of Spanish colonial revival offices and shops at 520–542 and 533–581 Ramona Street, just south of University Avenue. His Palo Alto residential work includes all the houses on Coleridge Avenue between Webster and Cowper Streets, as well as his own house at 1490 Edgewood Drive.

In the 1960s and '70s, he designed four buildings on the campus: the three John Stauffer laboratories for organic chemistry, physical chemistry, and chemical engineering of 1960 through 1966; and the Seeley G. Mudd Chemistry Building of 1977. He also taught in Stanford's architecture program from 1950 until 1972.

While Clark worked in many architectural forms, including ranch-style, streamline moderne, and commercial glass boxes, his signature style was Spanish eclectic, which is Palo Alto's basic and enduring architectural style. Characteristics include thick walls, blank front walls with small windows, tile roofs (sometimes shake or shingle), iron or plaster grilles, verandas, and arches. The houses he designed were generally L-shaped, had deeply recessed front doors, and large glass doors opening onto back patios that served as living rooms. Clark referred to this as an "economical style," and said he was inspired by Pedro de Lemos's Gotham Shop on Ramona Street and Allied Arts Guild in neighboring Menlo Park.

In 1922, Birge Clark married Lucile Townley, daughter of Stanford Professor Sidney D. Townley, an astronomer and mathematician. (They had met when Clark was designing the Townleys' house at 661 Cabrillo.) She had received a bachelor's degree in German at Stanford in 1918, and with her husband raised four children. She was an active volunteer in the American Red Cross, especially during World War II, and also in the PTA. She died in 1986.

Birge Clark lived and worked in Palo Alto until his death at 96, in 1989. When reflecting on his long and prolific career, he said, "I think it was better when mainly people stayed in one place, putting down roots and knowing everybody. Palo Alto was a family to me."

—Mandy MacCalla

In 1982, Clark was still practicing in his Palo Alto office. Photograph on the wall is of the Lou Henry Hoover House on campus.

SOURCES

Gauvin, Peter. "Birge Clark (1893–1989)." *Palo Alto Weekly* (25 May 1994).

Glover, Frederic O. "The Daring Young Men in the Tethered Balloons" and "Birge: After the War." *Sandstone & Tile* (Stanford Historical Society) 10, no. 3-4 (Spring/Summer 1986).

Kushman, Rick. "Birge Clark: the man behind the blueprints." *Palo Alto Weekly* (15 April 1994).

Weinstein, Dave. "Signature Style: Birge Clark California Colonial: Palo Alto's favorite architect mixed romance with realism." *San Francisco Chronicle* (5 July 2003).

An Architect Grows Up in Palo Alto: Memoirs of Birge M. Clark, FAIA. Privately published (September 1982).

PHOTOS

Early photos, Clark family collection; 1982 photo, Carolyn Caddes/Palo Alto Historical Association.

~ Charles K. Sumner

Between 1911 and 1930, Charles Kaiser Sumner designed more than 30 residences on the Stanford campus. While his commissions included an occasional office building, school, church, or country club, his Stanford houses are typical of his work, the bulk of which was subtly stylish housing for the comfortable middle class. His clients were business people and professionals, including a large number of Stanford professors, for whom he built houses both on and off campus.

Born Charles Sumner Kaiser in Wilkes-Barre, Pennsylvania, in 1874, he reversed the order of his middle and last names during World War I. He graduated with a degree in architecture from Columbia University in 1902, then traveled to Europe and the Middle East on a Perkins fellowship. His career began in New York City, where he worked in the firm of McKim, Mead & White during a period when it carried out some of its most important metropolitan commissions. He worked under Charles Follen McKim, whom he greatly respected and admired for his talent and dedication. McKim was the partner later responsible for designing Pennsylvania Station.

After a visit to the West Coast in 1906, Sumner moved to Berkeley, where he lived and practiced for 10 years. He built about 15 houses there, as well as the Claremont Club, taking shares in the club in lieu of a design fee. He also designed several buildings in Sacramento, including the multistory Farmers & Merchants Bank, and several large residences. In 1916, he moved to Palo Alto, where he designed about 90 buildings in town or on the Stanford campus. Although he lived on Palo Alto's University Avenue, his professional office was in San Francisco.

Sumner worked squarely within the eclectic movement but also mastered the details of many styles. He preferred the Craftsman, Tudor, and colonial revival models, as well as the occasional Beaux-Arts/Mediterranean revival structure. After the Spanish eclectic style swept into town—stimulated by George Washington Smith's 1925 design for the Pettigrew house at 1336 Cowper Street in Palo Alto—Sumner worked more and more in that style.

Sumner's residential designs reflect a certain formality, with distinct separations between public and private spaces, and space between servants and the served. His are houses for entertaining, with the typical ground-floor arrangement of reception hall and generous dining and living rooms. There is almost always room for a piano, and indeed on more than one occasion Sumner was asked to design a stand-alone music room addition. Stairs are positioned for privacy, either perpendicular to the view from the front entrance or tucked away into a niche to prevent a direct line of sight to the family spaces on the second floor.

Sumner was suspicious of the Modern movement. He said that the modern house, as a "machine for living," lacked "cheer and comfort," yet he applauded the movement's ideals of functionality and approved of its expression of function in interior design. Sumner generally provided built-in storage, such as cupboards and closets, as part of the composition of the interior spaces; he also included multiple bathrooms. His master bedrooms often had dressing areas with built-in dressing tables positioned to take advantage of light from well-placed windows. While there was often a butler's pantry, his kitchens were usually small and utilitarian servant spaces, as was typical for the period in which he worked.

Sumner believed that house, garden, and interior furnishings had to work together and that their design

Charles Sumner in an undated photo.

was a collaborative effort. He spoke respectfully of the landscape architect who brought his own "scale of spaces and proportions, his own tools and materials," and warned the building architect of the dangers of leaving "obstructions" in the way of landscape design. Sumner was more suspicious of the decorator and strictly limited his work. He believed the architect was to design the "interior architecture of walls and ceilings, cabinets, fireplaces, and staircases," and the decorator's province was "color, rugs, furnishings, and hangings." And, if the architect was "the executive in charge," a collaborative approach ensured that "the whole [was] made far lovelier than the sum of its parts," and the "pitfalls of disharmony" could be avoided.

The garden and its relationship to the house were an especially important element for Sumner, who believed that "it takes both house and garden to make a home." According to a former boarder who lived with the Sumners while attending Stanford, Sumner believed that "every room had to be suitable for an elderly lady to live in, with windows on two or even three sides if possible to look out at the gardens." He planned his own garden with great care, "each rose bush so many feet from the next."

Sumner wished to imbue his houses with "a feeling of permanence," meaning "reasonable, obvious strength and durability." The job of the architect was to "constantly take the trouble" to achieve beauty. Restraint was an important element of beauty: "composure...is the groundwork on which beauty rests." Composure was for Sumner the object of composition: "the process of composing and quieting a house's various parts, so that they appear happy and at peace together." Chief among the architect's tools for composition, including balance, scale, and symmetry, was proportion, the "magic key to beauty" in home design.

In addition to his residential work, Sumner designed the original Walter Hays Elementary School (since razed) in Palo Alto, the Los Altos Golf and Country Club, the Butte County Courthouse in Oroville, and the Rangers' Club for the National Park Service in Yosemite. He also designed Palo Alto's College Terrace Library, employing WPA workers in its construction.

Sumner was active in Palo Alto civic life. He served on the Palo Alto Planning Commission, and was one of the earliest backers of the University Avenue underpass. He and his wife, Alice, a watercolorist, were members of the Palo Alto Art Club (now the Pacific Art League). Through this club, he likely knew architects Pedro de Lemos, A. B. Clark, and Birge Clark.

Charles Sumner died in Palo Alto in 1948, after a long illness. Survivors included his wife, six children, and five brothers.

—GRACE HINTON

Original Walter Hays School, shown here in a 1924 photo, was replaced in the 1970s.

SOURCES

Author interview with Linda Williams of the Claremont Club (16 June 2003).

Buildings List [index to building permits as published in the *Palo Alto Times* (1893–1950s)]. Palo Alto Historical Association.

Charles K. Sumner [obit]. *Palo Alto Times* (26 May 1948).

Charles K. Sumner [obit]. *New York Times* (27 May 1948).

City of Palo Alto, *Historic Buildings Inventory.* Palo Alto Historical Association.

Gail Woolley interview with Dr. Ralph Tanner (14 May 1995).

Sumner, Charles K. "A Half-Hour Talk on House Design." Stanford University Press (1936).

Web sites: College Terrace Library, Pacific Art League, National Park Service, Walter Hays School.

PHOTOS

All, Palo Alto Historical Association.

By the 1970s, mature landscaping embraced the College Terrace Library.

College Terrace Library, one of many buildings Sumner designed in Palo Alto, opened in 1936.

El Escarpado Way: 'Biz Hill'

BYRON FEIG

During the 1920s, Stanford had a modest housing boom, the result of an increase in faculty and pressure for more places to live on campus. At the university's direction, Charles Moser, associate professor of civil engineering, surveyed the area of campus land known as San Juan Subdivision No. 3, including Gerona Road and Santa Maria as well as El Escarpado for housing lots.

Uphill from Gerona Road near Campus Drive, El Escarpado's short cul-de-sac comes as a surprise. Compared to the eclectic diversity of most other campus housing, here four Tudor period style houses are sited close together around a venerable oak tree. If it weren't for the street's Spanish name meaning *high escarpment* or *precipitous*, the houses might be in an English village. They share common elements—stucco and timbered exteriors, steeply pitched roofs, arched wooden doors, and small dormers—yet each house retains its own character.

Three (421, 445, and 450 El Escarpado) were designed as a unit in 1927 by Charles K. Sumner for faculty members in the new Graduate School of Business. Because of the preponderance of Business School faculty, the area became known as "Biz Hill." The fourth (at 430), by Binder and Curtis of San Jose, was built in 1929.

The three Sumner houses all have a wing at a right angle to the main house; 430 has a simpler floor plan and, unlike the other three, no gables. All have been carefully restored and updated.

Though the lots are all about an acre in size, the houses are clustered close to the street, with two shared driveways. As a result, all four properties have magnificent back gardens sloping down toward Campus Drive or Gerona. (The lower parts of 421 and 430 were subdivided in the 1940s and 1970s, respectively.) ❋

421 El Escarpado Way

BYRON FEIG

1927 ~ Tudor period style

ARCHITECT	OWNERS
Charles K. Sumner	Dowrie—White—McConnell

BY SOPHIA MCCONNELL

The house Charles Sumner designed for Professor George W. Dowrie and his wife, Lillian, cost about $19,000 to build. Not including the large half-basement and attic, the house contains about 4,000 square feet. The shallow-arched front door, framed in sandstone, opens to a hallway with the living room on the left, dining room on the right, and a study directly ahead. High ceilings and beautiful oak floors are found throughout the house, as are small-paned casement windows and paneled doors of solid wood.

In the sun-filled living room, two steps lower than the entry hall, windows on the three exterior walls balance interior daylight and give an airy feeling. At the far end, a large bay window offers a view of the side garden, rose bushes, and a sloping lawn. Glass doors to the front porch provide a view not only of the cul-de-sac's center (referred to by residents as "the circle"), but of the enormous trunk of an ancient deciduous oak tree growing in the lawn. On the living room's right-hand wall, the fireplace has an elegant and unusual molded-concrete mantel.

From the dining room, windows in the street-facing wall bring in views of the oak tree growing in the circle. While no particular architectural features define this room, a sharp eye can see a service button on the hardwood floor that rang a kitchen bell (no longer existing).

At the back of the entry hall is a study, altered from its original form, and to the right of this room stairs lead to the second floor. Halfway up, at a landing with a small closet, large windows overlook the rear garden. Because of the lot's slope, the second floor is half a floor higher from ground level, so backyard views are more wide-angled than those from the first floor.

Upstairs are three bedrooms. Directly above the living room are the master bedroom and bath. As with the living room, these rooms are down two steps. At the head of the stairs, a large bedroom on the front of the house has built-in bookcases on both sides of large windows looking out on the cul-de-sac's oak. A full attic is reached by a pull-down ceiling staircase.

The third bedroom, just to the left of the staircase, shares a bathroom with the middle one. Two windows overlook the rear garden, and from the closet two small attics are accessible.

Except for the mahogany-paneled downstairs study (remodeled in 1950) and the kitchen (remodeled in 1989), the rest of the house retains its original lath-and-plaster walls and ceilings; ceilings have an interesting texture rather than being smooth.

Owners and Occupants

~George W. Dowrie~

Dowrie, born in Pontiac, Illinois, in 1880, was professor of finance at the Graduate School of Business from its establishment in 1926 to 1946. He was a noted economist, with degrees from Lake Forest College (A.B., 1901), University of Chicago (M.A., 1907), and University of Illinois (Ph.D., 1913), and an honorary LL.D. from Lake Forest in 1941. In 1908, he married Lillian Otis.

George W. Dowrie

Dowrie served on the faculties of the universities of Illinois, Michigan, and Minnesota, then as head of the business school at Minnesota from 1919 until 1926. He was the author of many articles

From the front door, dining room with longcase clock is on right, open stairway behind. Arched door leads to a study.

Original fireplace, of molded concrete, has an unusual cutout pattern between the mantel and the firebox.

and a number of books on investing, banking, and finance. After retiring from Stanford, the Business School's first professor emeritus then taught at San Jose State for three years. Dowrie was active in community and university affairs, and his annual economic forecasts were a tradition with the Palo Alto Rotary Club. He died in 1964, survived by his wife and his son, Dr. James O. Dowrie.

~Charles Langdon White~

In 1949, the house was bought by Charles Langdon White and his wife, Mary Ruth Sanford White. Professor White, born in Denver in 1897, received his B.S. from Dennison University in 1920, his Ph.D. at Clark University in 1925, and an honorary Sc.D. from Dennison in 1942. He was at Clark, Pittsburgh, and Western Reserve before coming to Stanford in 1943 as professor of geography. He specialized in the relation of politics, economics, and population growth to geography and natural resources. During World War II, he played an important role in the language and area programs of Stanford's Army Specialized Training Program. By the late 1940s, geography had become a regular component of Stanford's curriculum, and in 1950 the Department of Geography was established, with Professor White as its head until 1954; he retired in 1962. (The department was discontinued in 1963.) White was the author and coauthor of numerous books, scholarly and scientific papers, articles, and book reviews. Mrs. White died in 1981, her husband in 1989.

In 1950, the Whites had the existing study enlarged, and several features of this room differ markedly from the rest of the house. The walls are dark wood paneling rather than lath and plaster. The ceiling is high and pitched, while ceilings in the rest of the house are flat. This room has more built-in cupboards and cabinets compared with others, and also a pull-down table/desk. A flagstone fireplace was added in one corner of the room, with a woodbox door to its right. Large 70-inch-square plate-glass windows on two walls replaced paned ones. Because of the sloping lot, an occupant looking out from these windows has the sense of being suspended over the garden. From the basement below the study, one can see that this addition has an unusual support beam: a railroad track.

~Harden McConnell~

In 1965, the Whites sold the house to Harden and Sophia McConnell. Harden McConnell, professor of chemistry, emeritus, received his B.S. from George Washington University in 1947 and his Ph.D. in from the California Institute of Technology in 1951. He did postdoctoral work in the Physics Department at the University of Chicago, then worked for Shell Development Company between 1952 and 1956. He returned to Cal Tech in 1956 as professor of chemistry and physics, and moved to Stanford's Chemistry Department in 1964. The McConnells raised three children at Stanford: Hunter, Trevor, and Jane.

During this period, the yard as well as some of the neighbors' yards served as stock farms for goats and sheep, dogs and cats. (Jane McConnell was a member of 4-H when she was young. She was also a member of the Stanford

Floor-to-ceiling living room window with arched French door faces small patio by entry.

Remodeling in 1989 updated kitchen while keeping 1920s-style cabinets.

Polo Club and is known to have ridden her horse on El Escarpado.) Hunter and Trevor used some subterranean region of the Frederick Terman (now Sweeney) property for a secret fort until Professor Terman kindly suggested that another location might be better.

The house has a large attic space as well as large closet areas, which are filled with children's toys and literally hundreds of Jane McConnell's books. Oddly, this attic has a faucet that was installed during World War II, apparently for fire protection purposes.

The kitchen, behind the dining room and to the right off the entrance hallway, was remodeled in 1989, with the McConnells' son Hunter as the contractor. The original dividing wall between the kitchen and the laundry area was removed, and the laundry facilities were placed in the attached garage. The kitchen was then expanded to more than 10 feet wide by 21 feet long, large enough to allow for a comfortable dining area at one end. Vinyl floors were replaced with random-plank oak floors. Crown molding added as part of the remodel is in keeping with the age of the house. Off the far end of the kitchen are a maid's room and bath. The pantry, which connects the kitchen to the dining room, was altered and updated in a style consistent with the rest of the house.

In 2002, a few exterior improvements and upgrades were made. The roof was replaced with flat cedar shingles over a plywood substructure for fire and earthquake resistance. New copper gutters were also installed. Remarkably, much of the original gutter and drain system that leads to rock-filled underground pits is still fully functional. Professor White had replaced the original oil heating system, but in 2000 a new forced-air gas furnace was installed. Water pipes under the house and in the garden were replaced during 2000–03, and the entire sprinkler system replaced in 2003.

Since the many windows in each room offer such varied views, it seems possible that Charles Sumner and the original owners carefully considered the landscaping of the surrounding garden, which includes several massive native oaks. The front garden comprises mainly lawn with two deciduous oaks: one in the lawn itself and another on the left side. An orange and a lemon tree also grow here. Until the 1970s, three tangerine trees also grew in the lawn at the side of the house. These trees along with the "orchard" plot designated in the original blueprints suggest the architect wanted to incorporate these fruits into the landscape.

In the rear garden, many paths terrace the sloping lot and create distinct garden beds, each with varying degrees of sunlight. Two more deciduous oaks grow here, as well as several smaller live oaks and a beautiful deodar cedar. This tree, now one of the taller ones, was once a living Christmas tree that came indoors. A birdbath in rough rocks attracts a variety of birds.

A latticed pergola built off the side yard on the right and a brick in-ground barbecue beside the pergola suggest that this area was used for social events. By the time the McConnells bought the house, the pergola had fallen into disrepair. However, they kept the tumbledown structure for quite some time because it supported a beautiful climbing rose. Eventually the side yard became home to Jane McConnell's 4-H project: dairy goats. A pen and shed encircled much of the area.

In the late 1980s, their son Hunter built a potting shed to replace the pergola. Its Tudor style appears as a miniature of the main house. The same climbing rose bush, with pale pink flowers, grows just off the side of this shed.

In 2003, Patti Hughes of Maison-du-Lac relandscaped the rear garden to take full advantage of its contours. The garden paths are bordered with rocks taken from building debris resulting from the 1989 earthquake. Automatic sprinklers irrigate the entire property. ❋

SOURCES

"Charles Langdon White" [biographical entry]. *American Men of Science,* 4th ed. (1968).

"Dr. Dowrie, noted educator, dies at 83" [obit and death notice]. *Palo Alto Times* (22 June 1964).

"Dr. George W. Dowrie: He will be first from business school to get emeritus rating." *Palo Alto Times* (4 June 1946).

Dowrie, George William [biographical entry]. *Who Was Who.*

McConnell, Harden. Curriculum vitae (1992).

Memorial Resolution: Charles Langdon White (1897–1989). Stanford University Academic Council.

Memorial Resolution: George W. Dowrie (1880–1964). Stanford University Academic Council.

McConnell, Hunter. Original remodeling plans (1989). Collection of Harden McConnell.

Sumner, C. K. Original house plans (1927). Collection of Harden McConnell.

PHOTOS

Dowrie, Stanford News Service; all others, Leni Hazlett.

430 El Escarpado Way

BYRON FEIG

1929 ~ Tudor period style

ARCHITECTS	OWNERS
Binder and Curtis	Sewall—Hurlbut—Estess —Mnookin—Schurman

BY DEEDEE SCHURMAN

Contractor William Short built this house for Dr. Edward C. Sewall, a professor in the School of Medicine; final cost was $20,766. The 3,753-square-foot house is two stories, with a small basement and an unfinished attic. Its redwood-framed mahogany front door opens into a spacious entryway that is highlighted by a beamed ceiling and a broad staircase to the second floor. Honduran mahogany was used throughout for doors, ceiling beams, bookcases, and the main staircase; framing is redwood, and floors are white oak.

To the left of the entry, French doors in a Tudor arch open to the 19- by 29-foot living room. A carved stone fireplace on the long outside wall is an impressive feature, and in each corner of the shorter walls is a floor-to-ceiling bookcase. The square-paned "true divide" metal windows have their original pull-down screens, and French doors open to the patio and back garden.

Through French doors to the right of the entry is the dining room with a bay window on the front wall.

Opposite the entry, a small study has a wall of bookshelves and French doors to the back garden. In this same area, an arched door and two steps down provide access to a half-bathroom, stairs to the unfinished basement, a door to the back patio, and (up two stairs) to the kitchen.

The kitchen, behind the dining room, is the only room in the house that has had any major upgrades, and those not until the 1970s. It still retains its butcher-block and Mexican tile counters, glass-fronted cabinets, ceramic cabinet knobs, and open shelving from that era. From the kitchen, stairs lead up to a bedroom and a bathroom, most likely used as maid's quarters but eventually a student rental. This bedroom has built-in drawers and several large closets. Other stairs lead from the kitchen down to the garage. A cold cabinet, still in use, is in the back entry.

In front hall, arched door next to imposing mahogany staircase conceals half-bathroom down two steps.

On the second floor are three bedrooms and two bathrooms. The 19- by 21-foot master bedroom, at the top of the stairs and above the living room, has a fireplace, a small sewing area, a sleeping porch, a large bathroom with shower and tub, and ample built-in storage space including drawers in the bedroom closet. The other two bedrooms are also large; one has a sleeping porch with a Murphy bed and access to the attic, the other a small balcony overlooking the street. Off the upstairs hallway are a broom closet and a floor-to-ceiling linen closet with multiple drawers and shelves.

From the house's obvious attention to detail and Dr. Sewall's comments on the original plans, it is clear that he was very involved in planning the house, and he added some unusual architectural and building concepts. For instance, an outside stairwell allows direct access to the basement, where there are a furnace and a dumbwaiter to the pantry in the kitchen. The garage also has a half-bath that workers could use without entering the house. The house's three full bathrooms have utility doors for easy access to the water pipes, and the floors of the three second-floor decks were covered in treated canvas; two remain intact. The original roof was made of pressed asbestos shingles and was called a "lifetime" roof; it lasted nearly 75 years. A wrought-iron S (for Sewall) on the chimney has been removed.

However, Dr. Sewall's most intriguing contribution is four "secret" cupboards where jewelry, silver servers, or other valuables can be stored. His handwritten note detailing the location and description of these cupboards has been handed down to each new owner.

The Architects

~Binder and Curtis~

William Binder was born in San Francisco in 1871. He acquired his architectural education by working as an apprentice, which was quite common at the time. His boss and mentor was George W. Page, a leading architect in San Jose. In 1895, Binder and Fairly Weiland opened a firm as partners; two years later, Binder set out on his own.

Binder (pronounced *Bender*) was the first local architect to use an electric elevator and to use iron- or steel-reinforced concrete in the construction of commercial buildings, both of which allowed for taller structures. He designed most of the San Jose movie houses, including Sid Grauman's Unique Theatre (1903), the Jose (1904), the T&D (1913), the Hippodrome (1919), and the neighborhood theaters the Hester (1927), now known as the Towne Theatre, and the Willow Glen (1933).

In the early 1900s, Binder had collaborated with T. S. Montgomery, one of San Jose's early developers. Binder's firm became the chief designer for Montgomery's downtown developments. In fact, most of the buildings on South First Street, from San Antonio Street to San Carlos Street originated in the Binder office. Only the Montgomery Hotel and the Twohy Building remain today; both are city landmarks. One of Binder's most architecturally beautiful buildings, built in 1923, is the former Christian Science Assembly Church at 72 North Fifth Street. Now called Le Petit Trianon, it is a popular auditorium for concerts.

Ernest Curtis was born in San Jose in 1889. His father was a builder, and he lived in one of the first houses built in the Naglee Park area of the city. Like Binder, Curtis apprenticed with George W. Page. Curtis worked for Binder as a draftsman until he joined the Army during World War I. Upon Curtis's return in 1918, Binder welcomed him as a full partner. They worked together until the late 1920s; when projects were few during the Great Depression, Binder went into semiretirement. From this point, designs were almost exclusively those of Curtis.

Beginning in the 1930s, Curtis drew plans for many luxury houses in the area. He used a variety of styles, such as Tudor in Naglee Park, neocolonial for the home of Sewell Brown in Los Gatos, and Spanish colonial for the home of Roy McCallum in Hollister, which was placed on the National Register of Historic Places in 1997.

Owners and Occupants

~Edward Cecil Sewall~

Dr. Sewall was born in 1875 in Portland, Oregon. He received his bachelor's degree from Stanford in 1898 and his medical degree in 1902 from Cooper Medical College, later acquired by Stanford as its School of Medicine. Before graduating, Sewall served as an instructor of ophthalmology at Cooper, and in 1907 became an assistant professor. He spent four years doing graduate work in Freiburg, Germany, and in London, Paris, and Vienna. Upon his return to the Medical School in 1912, he became associate professor of diseases of the ear, nose, and throat, and then clinical professor of surgery. He retired in 1940.

On April 10, 1957, the *Palo Alto Times* reported that Dr. Sewall had apparently killed himself in his bathtub using a .38-caliber revolver. Dr. Sewall, who was 81, had been in ill health for several months. He was survived by his wife, Amy Lunt Sewall; they had no children. She died in Palo Alto in 1972, aged 91.

Dr. Edward Sewall

Back of the house overlooks carefully tended garden with dining patio and broad lawn. Spreading oak casts shade; flowers and smaller trees add seasonal color.

~John Bingham Hurlbut~

Professor Hurlbut and his wife, Elizabeth Harrison Hurlbut, bought the house in 1958 and, apart from a year in England and Japan, lived there until 1975. He was born in Wisconsin in 1906, graduated with a bachelor's degree from UCLA in 1928, and earned his master's in political science at Stanford in 1929. He graduated in 1934 from Stanford Law School with one of the highest grade point averages up to that time.

He then spent three years in private practice. Returning to Stanford in 1937, he taught civil procedure, evidence, criminal law, contracts, and persons and domestic relations for 34 years. He was one of the first law faculty named to an endowed chair, the Jackson Eli Reynolds professorship, in 1959.

Affectionately known as the "silver fox," he was regarded as an excellent teacher by his students. In a 1970 *Stanford Law Review* issue honoring Hurlbut, Professor Harold Shepherd called him "a brilliant student, inspired and inspiring teacher, and one of the gentlest and kindest of men." Professor Samuel D. Thurman, then dean of the University of Utah College of Law, called Hurlbut "a master of Socratic dialogue."

Hurlbut was an avid sports fan and served as the faculty athletic advisor to the Pacific Coast Conference (now the PAC-10) and as vice president of the National Collegiate Athletic Association. For several years after his 1971 retirement, he lectured at Hastings College of Law, in San Francisco. He died in 1987, aged 81.

~Floyd Estess~

Dr. Estess and his wife Emily owned the house from 1975 to 1981. It was during their tenure that the house underwent its only major renovation. Soon after moving in, they converted the kitchen, two pantries, the laundry room, and a closet into a large kitchen with French doors to the back patio, and a new laundry room. This was and still is the only structural change made to the house since it was built, in 1929.

However, the Estesses made another major change: they subdivided the land and built a new house, addressed as 400 El Escarpado Way. In 1981, they sold 430 to Robert Mnookin and moved to the new house; it was bought in 1996 by the Center for Advanced Study in the Behavioral Sciences for its director.

Dr. Estess, born in 1921 in Sacramento, received his bachelor's degree from the University of California at Berkeley in 1945, and his medical degree from University of California at San Francisco in 1948. He completed his residency in psychiatry at Langley Porter Institute, San Francisco. From 1954 to 1968, Dr. Estess had a psychiatry practice in the Los Angeles area and served in the Department of Psychiatry at UCLA. In 1961, he earned a Ph.D. from the Southern California Psychoanalytic Institute.

In 1968, the Estesses moved to Northern California, and in 1973 he was appointed director of the adult and child psychiatric clinics at Stanford and clinical professor of psychiatry. He specialized in the treatment of depression. Dr. Estess died in 2001.

John B. Hurlbut

From the living room, arched French doors open to front entry, with a view to dining room through another arch.

~Robert Harris Mnookin~

Mnookin, a law professor, and his wife, Dale, bought the house in 1981 and occupied it with their two daughters until 1993. They did very little interior renovation or remodeling during their 12-year residency. However, extensive landscaping included a small arbor, a hot tub, lighting, and a well-designed and landscaped patio at the back of the house. Converting Mrs. Sewall's sewing room into a computer room and office brought the house into the late 20th century.

The Mnookins had intended to extensively remodel the downstairs of the house and add a family room, but the project was never begun because Professor Mnookin left for Harvard Law School.

Robert Mnookin was born in Kansas City, Missouri, in 1942. He earned his bachelor's and law degrees, both magna cum laude, from Harvard University in 1964 and 1968, respectively. Mnookin was a clerk for Judge Carl McGowan of the United States Court of Appeals, District of Columbia, in 1968–69 and clerk for Justice John M. Harlan of the United States Supreme Court in 1969–70. His areas of interest are negotiations and child advocacy. He was in private practice in San Francisco during 1970–72, then joined the Earl Warren Legal Institute at the University of California at Berkeley as director of the childhood and government project.

Mnookin came to Stanford Law School as a visiting professor in 1980–81, then joined the faculty in 1981. In 1987, he was appointed the Adelbert H. Sweet Professor of Law, and in 1988 he was named director of the Center on Conflict and Negotiation.

~David Schurman~

Dr. Schurman and his wife, DeeDee, bought 430 El Escarpado Way in 1993. They have done no interior renovation but have made extensive upgrades while maintaining the integrity and spirit of the original house. After nearly 75 years, the "lifetime" asbestos roof was replaced with shingles. To heat and cool the second floor, a second temperature-control system was installed in 1993, and the house has been retrofitted for earthquake safety. Much of the electrical wiring and interior plumbing has been upgraded as well.

Dr. Schurman was born in 1940 in Chicago. He received his bachelor's degree from Yale University in 1961 and his medical degree from Columbia University in 1965. After completing his orthopedic training, he was a postdoctoral fellow at UCLA from 1972 to 1973.

In 1973, the Schurmans and their two children moved to Stanford, where he joined the Medical School faculty as an assistant professor. Other than spending one year as a visiting scholar at Cambridge University and Strangeways Research Lab, Dr. Schurman and his family have lived at Stanford, where he is now professor of orthopedic surgery. ❋

Through two owners, the floral-patterned wallpaper and matching upholstered chairs in the dining room have remained unchanged.

SOURCES

"Amy Lunt Sewall" [obit]. *Palo Alto Times* (25 January 1972).

Douglas, Jack. "William Binder: San Jose's First Major Modern Architect." *Continuity: Preservation Action Council of San Jose Newsletter* 13, no. 2 (Spring 2002): 10–12.

Douglas, Jack. "Ernest Curtis: William Binder's Junior Partner Also Left Imprint on San Jose." *Continuity: Preservation Action Council of San Jose Newsletter* 13, no. 3 (Summer 2002): 8–10.

"Edward Cecil Sewall" [obit]. *Palo Alto Times* (10 April 1957).

Engelbrecht, Molly Hurlbut. E-mail correspondence with Marian Adams (14 September 2004).

Estess, Floyd [press release]. Stanford University Medical Center News Bureau (10 January 1973).

"Floyd Estess" [obit]. *Stanford Report* (2 May 2001).

"John B. Hurlbut, former law professor, dies" [press release]. Stanford University News Service (1 April 1987).

Memorial Resolution: Floyd H. Estess (1922–2001). Stanford Unversity Academic Council.

Memorial Resolution: John Bingham Hurlbut (1906–1987). Stanford University Academic Council.

"Mnookin—expert in both family law and dispute resolution—named to Adelbert Sweet Professorship at Stanford Law School" [press release]. Stanford University News Service (15 May 1987).

Robert Harris Mnookin. Curriculum vitae (1992).

Schurman, David. Curriculum vitae (May 2001).

PHOTOS

Sewall, Lane Medical Library; Hurlbut, Kee Coleman/Stanford News Service; all others, Rafael Fogel.

445 El Escarpado Way

MARY McCANN

1927 ~ Tudor period style

ARCHITECT	OWNERS
Charles K. Sumner	Jackson—Terman—Sweeney

BY SUSAN SWEENEY

Shortly after Professor J. Hugh Jackson arrived at Stanford in 1926 as professor of accounting in the Graduate School of Business, contractor Minton Co. built this three-story house with full attic for a total cost of about $28,000. It is built on a terraced slope, so the lowest level—not visible from the street—opens the back of the house to a series of graded gardens. The house's Tudor style shows principally in its half-timbered center gable, steeply sloped shingled roofs, and exposed beams above the window casements. Walls are of beige-painted rough-textured "California" stucco.

The heavy oak front door, set into a recessed stucco arch, is accented at eye level by a small iron grate and the original brass handle. The entry step is made of clinker bricks in an interesting irregular pattern; to the right of the house front, steps of the same brick lead to a rose garden and gazebo. Under spreading oak trees on the house's left side is a curved stone patio with a rustic stone fireplace. Trees shading the back garden include palm, redwood, oak, and birch; this area is bordered by a seasonal stream that flows into Lagunita.

The entry hall runs the depth of the house; at the back, three steps lead down to an arched door out to a small curved balcony and brick stairway to the back garden.

To the right of the entry, the living room also runs from front to back, overlooking the rose garden. Central to this 18- by 29-foot room is the molded-concrete fireplace. Outside, the chimney is decorated with a large metal J, a reminder of the house's first owner, J. Hugh Jackson.

To the left of the entry, the square dining room opens onto a terrace by the front door. Behind this room and overlooking the back garden is a wood-paneled library with built-in bookcases, file cabinets, card catalog drawers, and a gun cabinet now housing a replica Stanford Axe. Sconces beside the fireplace are etched with a redwood tree.

A butler's pantry with a service door to the front of the house joins the dining room and kitchen. Consistent with many houses of the time, there is a maid's room off the kitchen; it has a pine floor and a bed recessed into the wall. Buzzers in the upper hall and living and dining rooms were for calling servants.

A staircase leads to four bedrooms on the second floor. The stairs and banister are oak, as are the floors; the balusters are wrought iron. From the second floor hallway, a drop-down ladder leads to the attic, and a back stairway leads down to the kitchen.

In 1966, Frederick Terman and his wife, Sibyl, moved to 445 El Escarpado. (They had owned the house for several years before moving from their former house at 659 Salvatierra.) The Termans renovated the house significantly that year, when they retained Henry L. Blackard, AIBD, of Menlo Park to remodel the kitchen; plans included turquoise plastic laminate counters, which were popular at the time. A redwood deck was also added across the back of the house, with sliding glass doors replacing French doors in the living room and kitchen.

The Termans also added a modern wing to the back left side of the house; it included a student apartment on the lower level and a master bedroom suite on the main floor. The wing was built on an angle to best take advantage of passive solar energy. Terman added numerous electrical lines and multiple telephone lines, and an air-conditioning system. The final plans for this project show additional work,

In the living room, gently arched fireplace has a decorative wood surround, popular in the late 1920s.

First-floor library has built-in file cabinets and card catalog drawers as well as original brass sconces —one on each side of fireplace—etched with El Palo Alto, a Stanford (and Palo Alto) icon.

which was never completed.

Sibyl Terman decorated the house with Asian art. The playroom on the lower level below the living room was used for music lessons, and one of the large bedrooms on the second floor was converted to a study.

In 1984, James L. Sweeney, a professor in the School of Engineering, and his wife, Susan, bought the house. They engaged Palo Alto architect Roger Kelley Kohler to update the house and integrate the Termans' addition into the original design. Kohler and the Sweeneys relied heavily on Charles Sumner's original drawings for J. Hugh Jackson.

The sliding glass living room and kitchen doors were retrofitted with French doors, and the original kitchen and four small rooms (including a laundry room) became one large space for cooking, dining, and entertaining. A skylight brightens the eating area. Brick-paved terraces allow guests to wander through the backyard and around the side to the original stone patio, gazebo, and rose gardens.

The student apartment on the lower level of the Termans' addition was converted into a family room with a stairway leading to the kitchen area. The master bedroom suite became an office and a smaller bedroom suite. To match the original house's Tudor details, peaked roofs were added to the wing.

Over the years, 445 El Escarpado Way has been a gathering place for many social and Stanford-related events. During the Sweeneys' tenure, it has been on several house tours and was the site of a lecture on Provost Frederick Terman.

Imposing oak staircase has wrought-iron inserts between balusters. Arched door down three steps leads to back terrace.

The Owners

~J. Hugh Jackson~

Jackson was born in 1891 on a farm in Warren County, Iowa. He received his B.A. from Simpson College in 1912, and his M.B.A., with distinction, from Harvard University in 1920. In 1919, he became a CPA and taught accounting at the University of Oregon and the University of Minnesota.

He came to Stanford in 1926 and in 1931 became the second dean of the Graduate School of Business, a post he held until his retirement, in 1956. Additionally, he served as Stanford's acting comptroller from 1937 to 1940.

J. Hugh Jackson

It was during Dean Jackson's tenure that Stanford's Graduate

Back to the future: stucco and brick terraces replace utilitarian redwood deck added in the 1960s, opening the back of the house for entertaining.

School of Business achieved national recognition and respect in the business community. A highly successful teacher, Jackson demanded the highest standards of teaching from his faculty and served as a sympathetic and helpful mentor to countless students. In 1946 he was awarded the Diamond Key of the National Association of Teaching Certified Public Accountants "for distinguished contributions to the literature of accounting and auditing."

An active member of the community, Dean Jackson served on the boards of several banks, was president of the Stanford Bookstore, and was a member of the Palo Alto School Board and the Palo Alto Kiwanis Club. He remained active in academic affairs after his retirement and was a professor of business administration at the University of Santa Clara. He died in 1962.

He and his wife, Frederica Ann Harned, whom he married in 1914, raised two children while living at 445 El Escarpado. J. Hugh Jackson Jr. became a professor of management at the U.S. Naval Postgraduate School at Monterey, and their daughter, Charlotte Frederica, later Mrs. Erling A. O. Forland, lived in Palo Alto.

~Frederick Emmons Terman~

Terman, a man whose life can't be condensed into a few paragraphs, was born in Indiana in 1900 but spent most of his life on the Stanford campus. He was the son of Lewis Terman, "the psychologist who developed the Stanford-Binet Intelligence Quotient and who, in his early days, was influenced by Rousseau's theories on natural education."

The Terman family moved often, following Lewis Terman's career to Massachusetts, Southern California, and in 1910 to the Stanford campus, where he built a house at 761 Dolores. Fred Terman, encouraged to explore his own interests, spent his early years roaming the Stanford foothills, hunting rabbits, swimming in Lagunita, and fishing in Felt Lake. Sent to school at age 9, he advanced quickly and entered Palo Alto High School at age 13. He became a ham radio operator and by age 16 had his own transmitter, which he used to contact operators as far away as Texas.

As a Stanford undergraduate during World War I, he first studied mechanical engineering, then chemistry, in which he earned his bachelor's degree in 1920; he stayed to earn the additional degree of Engineer (the equivalent of a master's degree) in 1922. After completing his doctorate at M.I.T. in 1924, he was offered teaching positions both there and at Stanford, and chose to begin his career in California. Recuperating from tuberculosis and a ruptured appendix, he began teaching part-time in the Electrical Engineering Department in 1924 while working on his first book. He quickly moved up the ranks, becoming a full professor and head of the department in 1937. Among his many books, *Radio Engineering* (1932) is a classic in the field.

In 1928, Fred Terman married Sibyl Walcutt, a Stanford graduate student in psychology. They had three sons: Frederick, Terence, and Lewis. Mrs. Terman, an expert on the teaching of reading, was a proponent of the phonics system. Her book, *Reading: Chaos and Cure,* cowritten in 1958 with her brother Charles Child Walcutt, was widely used in the 1950s.

Terman, a popular teacher as well as an especially effective administrator, is also well known for his recognition of superior academic talent in his students and colleagues, and for encouraging them to take their ideas as far as they could. The Hewlett and Packard story is well known, but

Fred Terman in 1977, when he donated his house to the university.

Terman's encouragement and vision influenced other giants of Silicon Valley, too, among them Russell and Sigurd Varian, Edward Ginzton, and Bernard Oliver.

During World War II, Terman led the Radio Research Laboratory in Cambridge, Massachusetts. The lab, set up at Harvard under contract with the U.S. government, devised jammers for enemy radar and made tunable receivers for detecting and analyzing enemy radar signals. Terman also took the time to discuss with neighbors and friends at M.I.T. and Harvard ways to manage and promote great research universities.

Named dean of Stanford's School of Engineering in 1944, he returned to the campus in 1946 ready to take advantage of research and funding opportunities, particularly in the area of government-sponsored research. He continued efforts to attract talented engineering students and faculty, and to promote faculty research in such areas as communications and electronics, materials science, and aeronautical engineering. He also promoted links between engineering and other fields.

In 1955, Terman became provost (continuing as dean until 1959), and with President J. E. Wallace Sterling began the campaign to make Stanford a world-class university. He articulated a philosophy of "Steeples of Excellence": developing Stanford's strengths by attracting the best academic talent available. Many of these steeples, such as electrical engineering, materials science, aeronautics, and chemistry, supported new ventures based in Stanford's industrial park, building a strong connection between knowledge and industry. As provost, Terman also encouraged strong humanities and social science departments, building Stanford's history, political science, statistics, and computer science departments to national prominence.

Though Terman retired in 1965 at the mandatory age of 65, he continued with a busy schedule of international consulting, particularly in engineering education and university-industry relations. Much honored as the father of Stanford's modern School of Engineering and the architect of Silicon Valley, he received the university's Uncommon Man Award in 1978.

Two years after Sibyl Terman's death, in 1975, Frederick Terman bequeathed the house to the university to establish a fund in the School of Education in her honor. After his death, in 1982, the house was rented to Grant Barnes, director of Stanford University Press, and his wife, Irina, for the next year. In 1984, James and Susan Sweeney bought the house.

~James Sweeney~

Sweeney was born in Watertown, Connecticut, in 1944, and received his bachelor's degree from M.I.T. in electrical engineering in 1966 and his Ph.D. in

Two sons and their families gathered with Sibyl and Fred Terman for the 1965 dedication of Building 500 as the Terman Engineering Laboratory. From left, Terence, Marilyn, Sibyl, Frederick E., Kathleen, Patricia, Frederick, Sally, and Frederick W.

Engineering–Economic Systems (EES) from Stanford in 1971. His first faculty position was in EES, teaching economic analysis.

During the 1974 energy crisis, he took a two-year leave to join the newly established U.S. Federal Energy Administration in Washington, D.C. After returning to Stanford, he focused professionally on economic policy and analysis, particularly in energy, natural resources, and the environment.

He has served as chair of EES, and of the merged Department of Engineering–Economic Systems and Operations Research. Three years later, when it merged with the Department of Industrial Engineering–Engineering Management to create the Department of Management Science and Engineering, Sweeney returned to full-time teaching and research in this new department.

Professor Sweeney has been involved in several Stanford and outside organizations involved in energy modeling and economic policy research. Currently, he is board president of Stanford Campus Residential Leaseholders, the organization responsible for local governance of the Stanford residential community.

While in graduate school at Stanford, Sweeney met and married Susan Van Every, a graduate student in the School of Education. Their four children grew up in the house, which the Sweeneys have also shared with their parents. Susan Sweeney's father, Kermit Van Every, was a Stanford alumnus, having received his undergraduate and graduate degrees in the School of Engineering.

Susan Sweeney runs her own company, Conference Consultants. She is also executive director of the California Consortium of Education Foundations, and serves on various community boards. ❋

SOURCES

Gillmor, C. Stewart. *Fred Terman: Building a Discipline, a University, and Silicon Valley.* Stanford University Press (2004).

Glover, Frederic O. "Fred Terman's Paper Trail: A Goldmine of Scientific Research." *Stanford Historical Society Newsletter* (Winter 1979): 10–13.

"Lewis Terman." *Dictionary of American Biography* Supp. 6 (1956–1960).

Memorial Resolution: Frederick Emmons Terman (1900–82). Stanford University Academic Council.

Memorial Resolution: J. Hugh Jackson (1891–1962). Stanford University Academic Council.

Memorial Resolution: Lewis Madison Terman (1877–1956). Stanford University Academic Council.

"Sibyl Walcutt Terman" [obit]. *San Francisco Chronicle* (26 July 1975).

"Sibyl Walcutt Terman" [obit]. Stanford News Service (24 July 1975).

Sweeney, James. Curriculum vitae (2004).

Terman, Frederick Emmons. Papers, SC 160. Stanford University Archives.

Terman, Sibyl, and Charles Child Walcutt. *Reading: Chaos and Cure.* New York: McGraw-Hill (1958).

Villard, O. G. Jr. "Frederick Emmons Terman, 1900–1982." *Biographical Memoirs,* National Academy of Sciences 74 (1998): 308–331.

PHOTOS

House drawing, Mary McCann (2001); Jackson, Stanford Archives; Terman photos, Stanford News Service; all others, Leni Hazlett.

450 El Escarpado Way

BYRON FEIG

1927 ~ Tudor period style

ARCHITECT	OWNERS
Charles K. Sumner	Hotchkiss—Dodds—Kimpton —Krauskopf—Lyman—White

BY NATALIE AND DAVID WEBER
PHYLLIS AND ROBERT WHITE

Professor W. E. Hotchkiss chose Charles K. Sumner to be the architect for his house on a lot of almost a full acre on a cul-de-sac just off Gerona Road. This lot extends down to a drainage channel from the Stanford hills and to a utility road. Construction specifications and plans, dated June 1927, are for a structure including four family bedrooms, two maid's rooms, five baths, and a three-car garage. The construction price was $33,583 for a house of 5,243 square feet and garage of 535 square feet.

The house entrance faces north northwest. Two notable oak trees on the lot influenced placement and perhaps orientation of the house. In fact, the plans specify that the house be located "with reference to" an old oak tree that is still visible through the tall window above the stair landing. The house's exterior is cream-colored, slightly textured stucco with rust red window accents. Most of the gables have sections of rustic redwood clapboard. On the back of the house, window lintels have adzed and stained wooden decoration. The lintel over the front entrance is especially thick for stylistic accent. The steep roof still has its original flat red tiles laid like slate.

The house is reached by a circular drive. A stone path leads to a semicircular raised area of tile edged with brick by the front door. The front door is set into a gently curved elliptical arch, a shape also used for the top of the front door and for entrances into principal rooms. This design motif, one of Sumner's hallmarks, is also seen in the gentle barrel ceiling of the upstairs hall.

The floor plan is asymmetrical, with the living room projecting out at an angle from the base of a U-shaped plan. The entry hall, wide and deep, leads to the living room on the left, the dining room on the right, and a bedroom wing straight ahead. The gracious living room, 20 by 28 feet, is two steps below the entry hall; it is notable for a bookshelf alcove at the entry end and—through glass doors at the far end of the room—a decorative shallow balcony with wrought-iron railing.

From the entrance hall, a narrow hallway leads to bedroom 1 and a bath used by Professor Hotchkiss. It continues past redwood storage cabinets to a study area and an enclosed sleeping porch. The study has a fireplace, built-in bookshelves, and a window seat; its walls are board-and-batten paneling. A pocket door can close off this entire wing beyond the bedroom.

The dining room, to the right of the entry, has two corner china cabinets with leaded-glass doors. At the back of the dining room is a garden room, which can be closed off by folding glass-paned double doors. The kitchen is at the front of the house beyond the dining room; stairs lead from it to the second floor. Past the kitchen is a utility/laundry room. Off this room are a maid's room and bath and back stairs leading to another maid's (or student's) room and bath, and a large area over the three-car garage. These rooms have been rented to students over the years. Outside the laundry room is a tiled area enclosed by a 6-foot stucco wall.

The open main staircase is a highlight of the house, with ornamental iron balusters. At the landing, a very tall window (with a built-in window seat) frames the trees beyond. At the head of the stairs is bedroom 2, which has

Stucco house, tile roof, shade umbrella, and pots of geraniums give back patio off the garden room a Mediterranean look.

Arches in front hall and over doorway frame garden room at the back of the house.

an interesting bed alcove, a bay window (with a view of the big oak), and a built-in desk. There is a bath across the hall. An unfinished attic, over the downstairs bedroom, bath, and study, opens off this bath. The attic is divided into two areas separated by a door and a step, and lighted by a small dormer window. This area, once rented to a student, provides generous storage space.

Bedroom 3, above the entry hall and dining room, is reached through glass-paned double doors. It has built-in bookcases on either side. Originally, a bathroom off this bedroom also opened into bedroom 4. In the upstairs hall were linen cabinets. Over the kitchen, bedroom 4 has windows looking front, side, and rear. An enclosed sleeping porch with canvas floor opened off this room, but now is incorporated into it.

Fireplaces in the living room and paneled study are completely different in design. The living room one is formed by three segments of light-colored concrete, with bas-relief classical design elements and a shallow mantel. The fireplace in the study is faced with square red tiles set in a rich-toned wood frame with moderate-depth mantel.

Window in recessed arch at stair landing overlooks old oak in side garden; in the window seat, a three-dimensional art form rests comfortably.

All windows are multipane casements, most of iron, but some of wood. Most windows had retractable roller screens of bronze wire, no longer functional.

In addition to bells from outside entrances, there were others: dining room floor push buzzer to the kitchen, second-floor hall to the kitchen, living room to kitchen and to the study, bedroom 1 to kitchen and study, and a speaking tube from bedroom 1 to the study. A pass-through from the side hall to bedroom 1 was just large enough to handle a small tray, perhaps for delivering mail or breakfast. A similar pass-through is found between the upstairs hall and bedroom 3.

For convenient wood storage, outside doors enabled delivery of wood to boxes in the living room and study. A small utility basement beneath the entrance hall holds the hot-air furnace and the water heater. Several rooms had an auxiliary system of electric wall heaters with large coils.

At several places on the property are large segments of original Quad buildings. A pile of such material existed well after the 1906 earthquake, and campus residents could take what they wished for their properties. On the back patio is a bench made from a cornice.

Off the garden room, a large brick patio has a sweep of lawn beyond. To the rear of the living room is a hedged-in circular area with a large oak in the center. From here, two paths led down to a drainage ditch, crossed by a wooden footbridge that was later swept away by heavy rains. A pre-1950 garden shed hides amid the shrubbery well away from the house.

The Owners

~WILLARD E. HOTCHKISS~

During 1925–27, Hotchkiss and his wife, Irma, with their two children rented the house of Professor Hempl on Cabrillo (later Santa Ynez) while this house was being built. They occupied the new house only from 1927 to 1931, though they retained ownership until 1937.

Willard Hotchkiss

Hotchkiss was a brilliant student at Cornell, graduating in 1897 and earning his Ph.D. in 1905; he also studied in Europe. From 1905 until 1925, he taught at Northwestern University, where he specialized in industrial management and personnel, the last four years serving as dean of its business school. He was a visiting professor in political science at Stanford during 1915–16.

Brought back to Stanford in 1925, Hotchkiss was the founding dean of Stanford's Graduate School of Business, appointed for five years. He actually had devoted "most of his time to the practical application of his expert knowledge, having among his clients such enterprises as the National Industrial Federation of Clothing Manufacturers, the Institute of American Meat Packers, and the United States Coal Commission." After a one-year leave during 1931–32, Hotchkiss resigned to become president of the Armour Institute of Technology.

From 1932 to 1937, Alfred E. Clegg and his wife, Helen, rented the house. With them lived their two sons and two daughters, and at one time Mrs. Emma Horner, who served as cook. "Alf" Clegg had no Stanford connection, though three of his children attended the university.

~JOHN W. DODDS~

In 1937, Dodds and his wife, Marjorie, bought the house for $31,650. He was born in Grove City, Pennsylvania, in 1902, and received his A.B. from the College of Wooster in 1924, followed by a master's and Ph.D. from Yale in 1927 and 1932, respectively. It was there that he met another graduate student, Marjorie Jane Krantz, whom he married in 1928. Before coming to Stanford in 1937, he taught at the University of Pittsburgh.

Dodds was professor of English and, from 1942 to 1948, served as dean of the School of Humanities. In 1948, he founded and became director of Special Programs in the Humanities, an administrative unit his successor, William Clebsch, called "the incubator for hatching many innovative programs in the university." Among his many roles outside the university, Dodds was an amateur actor, was president of the Western College Association, chaired the editorial board of the *Pacific Spectator* literary magazine, and helped develop and promote educational television in the 1950s and '60s. He retired in 1967 and died in 1989.

The Doddses and their two sons lived in the house until 1947, when they moved to their new house at 729 Frenchman's Road.

~LAWRENCE A. KIMPTON~

Professor Kimpton and his wife, Marcia, bought the house and lived here from 1947 to 1950. He was born in

To the right of the front entry, another arch marks the entrance to the dining room.

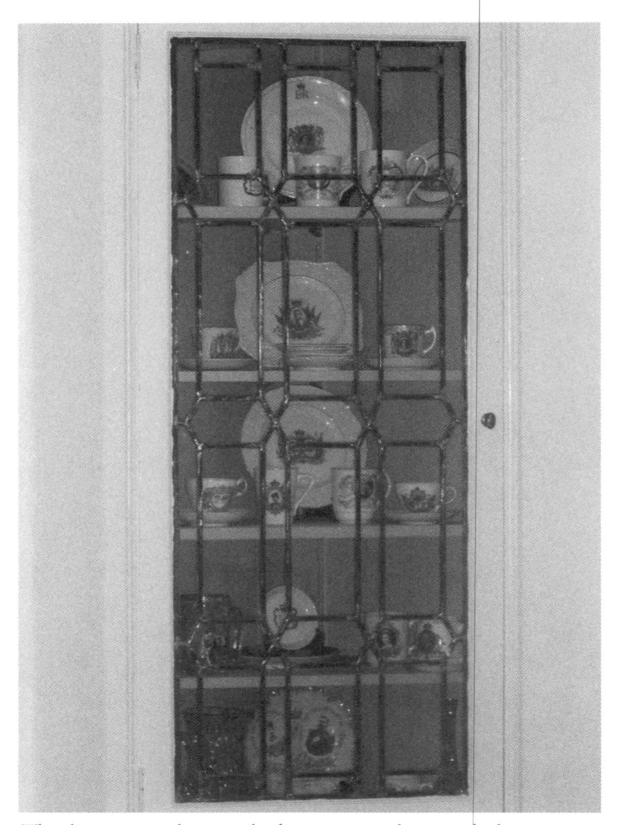

The dining room has two built-in corner cabinets, which retain their original leaded-glass doors.

Kansas City, Missouri, in 1910, and earned his A.B. from Stanford in 1931 and M.A. in 1932. After filling various positions at the University of Chicago, he returned to Stanford as dean of students and professor of philosophy. Three years later, the Kimptons returned to the University of Chicago, where he served as vice president for development and, from 1951 to 1960, as president.

~Konrad Bates Krauskopf~

With his wife, Kathryn, and their four children, Krauskopf lived in the house from 1950 to 1967. He was born in Madison, Wisconsin, in 1910; he earned his A.B. in chemistry from the University of Wisconsin in 1931 and two Ph.D. degrees: in chemistry from UC Berkeley in 1934 and in geology from Stanford in 1939. Krauskopf was instructor from 1935 to 1939, then assistant and associate professor before becoming professor of geochemistry in 1950. From 1943, he simultaneously served as geologist for the U.S. Geological Survey, and from 1960 as associate dean of the School of Mineral Science, later (1962) Earth Sciences. Kathryn McCune Krauskopf worked for some years as a counselor at Jordan Junior High School; she died in 2001. One child, Frances Conley, became a professor of neurosurgery at Stanford.

Concrete fireplace has molded classical elements including pilasters on each side of hearth.

The parents used the first-floor screened sleeping porch as their bedroom, while the children occupied the upstairs bedrooms. Two of the daughters were married at the house. The three rooms in the garage wing were regularly rented to students. Except for a few changes in the student rooms, the Krauskopfs made no significant alterations in the house during their ownership. Apparently the Krauskopf children built a fish pond, long since abandoned, on the lower part of the property. By 1967 the children had moved out, so the house was sold. Professor Krauskopf died in 2003.

~Richard Wall Lyman~

Lyman and his wife, Elizabeth (Jing), owned the house from 1967 to 1981, although they only lived there during the first four years with their four children. Lyman, born in Philadelphia in 1923, received his A.B. from Swarthmore in 1947, and M.A. and Ph.D. in history from Harvard in 1948 and 1954, respectively. He came to Stanford in 1958 from Washington University in St. Louis and from 1962 was professor of history. From 1964 to 1966, he was associate dean of the School of Humanities and Sciences, and from 1967 he was provost until being named president in 1970. He retired in 1980 to become president of the Rockefeller Foundation, returning eight years later to become director of the Institute for International Studies.

Jing Lyman attended Putney School in Vermont and received her A.B. from Swarthmore in 1947. After a year at Shady Hill Teachers Training School, she taught carpentry for two years. At Stanford, she was an active "career volunteer" involved in community service, fair housing, and women's opportunities.

In 1967, when Lyman became provost, they bought the house for $60,000 (and sold it 14 years later for seven times as much). They lived here until shortly after he became president. Though they had thought they could continue to live in this house they loved and use Hoover House for entertaining, after three months they consolidated in the president's residence.

In a published interview of November 1970, Jing Lyman commented that 450 El Escarpado "absorbs large groups perfectly...the house and garden easily handle 150 guests, and its setting on a wooded knoll provides privacy."

Student protests on campus in the Vietnam War era led to the need for exterior lighting for protective purposes. An electronic system provided a "hot line" to the campus security force, and a special fire alarm system was wired directly to the campus fire station. A wire strung around the perimeter of the backyard, installed by electrical engineering professor Bernard Widrow and his students, would ring an alarm if broken by an intruder.

Even with those precautions, protesters came at times to the cul-de-sac. In the spring of 1970, the Lymans were having a major reception for the incoming and outgoing deans of Humanities and Sciences, with President Pitzer and hundreds of other senior members of the faculty and administration on hand. Many students picketed the house, creating a gauntlet on El Escarpado through which those invited to the reception had to walk. That evening, a Coke bottle filled with red paint was thrown through the back kitchen window, just missing a guard who was taking a coffee break, creating a dreadful mess when it smashed against the refrigerator. Much later that night two rocks were hurled through the windows of the upstairs sleeping porch, which Jing and her daughters used as a sewing room. No one was in the room at the time.

~Ten Years of Tenants~

From 1971 to 1981, six families rented the house, among them Robert R. Augsburger and his wife, Jean Ann, who stayed during 1971–73. Augsburger was Stanford's vice president for business and finance. George P. Shultz and his wife, Helena (Obie), occupied the house during 1975–76. A former dean of the University of Chicago's Graduate School of Business, Shultz had served as U.S. secretary of the treasury (1972–74) before his 1974 appointment to the faculty at Stanford's Graduate School of Business. He served as U.S. secretary of state from 1982 to 1989. A subsequent tenant inflicted damage that required major renovation. Although the Lymans had looked forward to moving back to the house once his Rockefeller duties ended, housing costs in New York were such that they needed to sell it.

Richard W. Lyman in September 1970, after being named president of Stanford.

~Robert L. White~

In 1981, the Lymans sold the house to Professor White and his wife, Phyllis, who were moving to campus after 21 years in Los Altos Hills. White was born in Plainfield, New Jersey, in 1927 and received his B.A., M.A., and Ph.D. in physics from Columbia University. In 1952 he married Phyllis Lillian Arlt of Ridgewood, New Jersey, a graduate of Wellesley College. They have four children, two of whom graduated from Stanford and became physicians. Only the two youngest, Christopher and Matthew, still lived at home when the family moved in.

Upon receiving his Ph.D., Professor White joined the research staff of Hughes Research Laboratories in Southern California. From 1961 to 1963, he was head of the magnetics department of General Telephone and Electronics Laboratory in Palo Alto. In 1963, he came to Stanford with joint appointments in electrical engineering and materials science, becoming chairman of the Electrical Engineering Department in 1981 and the first holder of the William E. Ayer Professorship in Electrical Engineering. His research was in solid state physics, especially magnetics, and in neural prostheses that focused on a cochlear implant, called by some "the bionic ear." From 1987 to 1990, White was director of the Exploratorium in San Francisco. Returning to Stanford in 1991, he founded and became director of the Stanford Center for Research on Information Storage Materials. He has been involved in several high-tech start-up companies.

When Professor White was chairman of Electrical Engineering, the house's generous living room, patio, and lawns were the site of many large receptions and social events for faculty and students. The back patio is a favorite site for small summer parties. In recent years, the house has echoed with the voices of the Whites' seven grandchildren, who love to visit the house, climb its staircases, and play in the trees and tree house. In June 2002, the Whites' children hosted a 50th wedding anniversary party for their parents on the patio for more than 100 family and friends.

Over the years, the use of some of the rooms has changed. Early occupants used the first-floor wing as a master bedroom suite. The Whites use it as a TV/sitting room and guest bedroom. The former study is a project room, and the first-floor sleeping porch serves as Professor White's home office.

ALTERATIONS AND REMODELING

Extensive alterations have been made to maintain or improve aspects and functions of the house. Over time, the tile roof had developed fissures, and consequent rain damage necessitated extensive repairs in some areas. The 1989 Loma Prieta earthquake hit the campus hard, but the house sustained only minor damage—none to the chimney or foundation. However, water in the basement and pooling in the patio after heavy rains continued to be a problem. In 2000, the Whites fixed the water problem by installing pipes in ditches in the patio and lawn area to divert the water downhill toward the drainage ditch below.

The Whites have done extensive interior redecorating over the years: repainting, and replacing all window coverings and all lighting fixtures except the one in the downstairs front hall. In an antiques shop, Phyllis White found two crown-shaped wrought-iron electric chandeliers from another 1927 house; these were painted, rewired, and installed over the main staircase and in the downstairs study.

The Whites replaced the old black-and-white vinyl tiles in the garden room with terra-cotta tiles. Architect Frank Prendergast designed a major renovation in 1993 to the central section of the second floor: bedroom 3, the current master bedroom and its closet and bath, were enlarged; bedroom 4 was enlarged by combining it with the sleeping porch; and a half-bath was added. The contractor was Alexander Wert, who had been raised on the campus.

In 1999, a second major renovation by the same architect and contractor modernized the kitchen and breakfast area (the Lymans remodeled it in 1967, installing a service island and turquoise Formica countertops). The room was stripped to the studs, completely rewired, and reinforced with new supporting beams. (This work exposed wall drawings by the Lyman children.) Recessed lighting was installed in the ceiling, and hardwood floors replaced the old vinyl. The breakfast area was expanded and made brighter and more open. Granite countertops, a large island, new white cabinets, and topaz-colored walls all make an airy, welcoming, and functional kitchen. A tambour door in a counter corner hides small appliances. The stove was restored to gas, as in the original plan. A pocket door replaced the old tambour door to the utility area.

The Whites have many interesting works of art in the house. Bay Area artists such as Sam Francis, Nathan Oliviera, Ron Davis, and Cathy Coombs are represented, as well as Asian art items in several media. The Whites continue to add art objects from their frequent overseas trips.

LANDSCAPING

Initially, and still today, the garden has a quite remarkable variety of trees, though it is certain only that two large oaks on the east side were there in 1927, since their locations are marked on the original plans. The large oak in the rear, in the middle of what Jing Lyman called the Hidden Garden, probably also predates the house.

Robert White revitalized the old red climbing roses against the rear of the garage, which again bloom spectacularly, as do several old camellia bushes. Wisteria makes a lavender canopy climbing high over the trees along the back boundary. The Whites also planted wisteria on the house wall by the patio, as well as more climbing roses. Several strawberry trees, a tall deodar cedar, and European birch are important landscape elements. Four sycamores mark the corners of the patio. To the left of the house, some of the exotic plants such as bamboo, cactus, and citrus planted in the early years still remain.

During the years when the house was rented, the trees and shrubs grew rampantly. Shortly after moving in, the Whites took more than 20 truckloads of garden debris to the dump, and later on they had to remove a dangerously leaning blue spruce in the front entry area and replace it with a fir tree.

The Whites undertook two major landscaping projects. In 1987, the rear lawn area and the area in front of the house

In October 1970, Jing Lyman relaxes in the backyard of 450 El Escarpado with two of her four children, sons Tim (left) and Christopher (Cricket), and the family dog and cat. Three months later, the Lymans moved to Lou Henry Hoover House.

were redesigned and planted by Dick Seiler of Roger Reynolds Nursery, and a year later the Whites added a rose garden outside the den, near the back patio. In 2000, a second project, by Landsystems, entailed replanting the area by the driveway with sun-loving azaleas and vinca ground cover. The large area to the left of the house near the driveway was opened up and landscaped with a sweeping stone walk and plantings of rhododendrons, azaleas, hydrangeas, and lilies. A stone bench, a remnant of a Stanford building destroyed in the 1906 earthquake, is set against an oak tree. In 2002, Robert White replanted the area outside the front door with azaleas, nandinas, camellias, and pierises; the metal sculpture in a gravel area outside the front entrance is by Michel Melhuse. Professor White also planted the area between the back lawn and the neighbors beyond with shade-loving plants and built a low stone wall in front. In 2003, he built a new tree house beyond the back lawn for his grandchildren, who e-mailed him suggestions for its design. ❋

SOURCES

Augsburger, Robert. Conversation with authors (December 1998).

Clegg, Kay. Conversation with the authors (September 1998).

House plans, 450 El Escarpado, 8 sheets (1927). Stanford University Maps and Records.

House specifications. Office of Plant Services Records, SC 123, Box 4B, Folder 10, Stanford University Archives.

Krauskopf, Konrad, and Kathryn Krauskopf. Conversation with the authors (November 1998).

Lyman, Richard W., and Jing Lyman. Conversation with the authors (December 1998).

Memorial Resolution: John Wendell Dodds (1902–89). Stanford University Academic Council.

Memorial Resolution: Konrad Bates Krauskopf (1910–2003). Stanford University Academic Council.

"New president is an historian," *Stanford Observer* (October 1970): 3.

"Richard W. Lyman Reflects on His Life and the Turbulent '60s and '70s." *Sandstone & Tile* (Stanford Historical Society) 28, no. 2 (Spring/Summer 2004): 3–17.

"Stanford Graduate School of Business" [Willard E. Hotchkiss]. *Stanford Illustrated Review* 26, no. 9 (June 1925): 488.

White, Robert. Curriculum vitae.

PHOTOS

Hotchkiss and Lyman photos, Stanford News Service; all others, Margaret McKinnon.

440 Gerona Road

(446 Foothill, 440 Foothill)

BYRON FEIG

1928 ~ Spanish eclectic period style

ARCHITECT	OWNERS
Charles K. Sumner	Lee—Bunker—Glaser—Dement

By Natalie and David Weber

Architect Charles K. Sumner made a major impact upon faculty residences on the Stanford campus, and this one, designed and built in 1928 for Dr. Russel V. and Dorothy Lee, is one of his most distinctive, in scale and plan. The imposing entry and the many generous rooms show that Sumner was a skilled architect who knew the needs of his remarkable clients and their family.

On June 7, 1926, the Stanford Board of Trustees authorized a university-faculty lease to Dr. Lee for lots 12 and 13 (a total of 6 acres) of San Juan Subdivision No. 3. Dr. Lee received this double lot with support from Chancellor Emeritus David Starr Jordan, who, like Stanford presidents Ray Lyman Wilbur and later J. E. Wallace Sterling, was a patient of Dr. Lee's, as were the Herbert Hoover family and many of Stanford's faculty.

Sumner completed the design of the 4,000-plus-square-foot house in January 1928, with major guidance from Dorothy Lee. It was constructed during the next several months at an estimated cost of $25,000. Nearby was the house of physics professor David Webster, built in 1923 (the first on Gerona, at 576), as well as those of Eliot Mears (593) and Walter Miles (607), both built in 1926.

The Lees, with their five children, moved from Palo Alto to the campus sometime in 1928, and that year's *Stanford Register* listed them as living at the house's first address, 446 Foothill Road, which swept to the north of the house. A drawing for "change of alignment" in late 1931 shows existing and proposed routes around the house. The new road was built by chain gang prisoners in striped clothing, who were given drinks by the Lee boys. By 1931, the university had renumbered the house as 440 Foothill, an address it kept until 1940; that year the *Stanford Register* shows the address as 440 Gerona.

The lot sloped upward from the east corner and north-end driveway entrance to the south end. (The property today is about 2 acres, but it originally included land on the southeast side that was leased to Dr. D. Vernon Thomas for a new house, as well as land taken for the realignment of the road and for another house to the north.) One of the original two venerable valley oaks *(Quercus lobata)* still exists today, in breathtaking magnificence, on the living-dining-kitchen side of the house. A circular gravel driveway past the front door has a large evergreen magnolia tree in the center.

The house's architecture is regarded as Spanish eclectic, a style popular in California between about 1915 and 1940. The many arches suggest a simplified Moorish design, though they seem more Gothic in outline. The house's exterior is dusty buff stucco. The roof is of clay tile; it was said that all of the tiles were handmade by workmen who molded the clay over their thighs. (Some other tile-roofed houses in the vicinity offer up the same story.)

Brick steps lead to the small porch and front entrance. Heavy steel I-beams invisibly support the first and second floors. First-floor spaces include the entrance hall, living room, study, dining room, pantry, and kitchen, as well as a maid's room with bath, and a porch off a paved service yard. (For many years, Mrs. Zenna Higgins, as maid/cook, lived there with her daughter.) Attached to the house beyond the maid's room was a large two-car garage. The living room wing and the maid's room–garage wing are aligned, more or less north-south. However, the central segment with the dining room and kitchen is not at a right angle to the wings, which creates interesting visual relationships.

Front exterior, shown in 1945, has changed little in 60 years. Entrance is in tower at left; row of windows on right is sleeping porch.

The hexagonal entrance hall is one of the house's most striking features. From a small foyer inside the front door, two steps lead up to the hall. It is 26 feet tall and nearly 17 feet across, with a sweeping curved stair extending to the second floor. The stairway has oak railings and balusters; graceful iron grilles fill the spaces between. Halfway up the stairs, four tall arched windows bring light into the entry; their lower segments open outward.

Off the entry is a coat closet beneath the staircase; another door placed deeper under the stair leads to a washroom. On the hall's left side, an 11- by 12-foot hall extension opens to the living room through wood-paneled French doors and to the garden terrace through glass ones. Arches are found in many first-floor doors and windows, as well as in the living room's simple fireplace design. When the Lees lived in the house, a painting of a kneeling American Indian by Victor Arnautoff hung above the fireplace.

In the center of the house, the dining room opens to a tiled loggia on the driveway side, and to a brick terrace toward the pool and garden. The study also has a fireplace. Except for oak floors in the entrance hall, living room, dining room, and study, downstairs floors were pine and were originally covered with linoleum. Off the service porch are a clothes chute and a dumbwaiter between the first and second floors.

Downstairs ceilings are 8 1/2 feet high, except for the living room (down two steps); its ceiling is just over 11 feet, with two lateral and many longitudinal plastered beams. The room measures 20 by 35 feet, with French doors leading to the backyard to the southwest and to the garden to the southeast. In total, 13 doors on this floor lead outdoors.

On the second floor are five bedrooms, a children's study, a sewing room, and what the plans called a "deck (canvas)" over the garage. In one of the middle bedrooms, Dr. Lee painted maps of the world on two walls to help educate the children. There are three full baths. Floors are oak, and ceilings are 8 feet high. The house's many steel casement windows were equipped with roller screens in vertical guides, quite typical of the era.

Ancient valley oak on south side of house is probably several hundred years old.

A large concrete-floored basement extends under much of the house. This area was divided into a sunken room for the hot-air furnace and hot-water heater, a storeroom (now with a second hot-water heater), a "man's room," and a large central playroom with an 8-foot ceiling, a fireplace, and three large windows.

On the playroom walls, "Wolo" Trutzschler (1902–89) painted murals. (Baron Wolff Erhardt Anton Georg Trutzschler von Falkenstein acquired the nickname Wolo because his sister had trouble pronouncing his name.) For many years, he worked as a caricaturist-columnist for the *San Francisco Chronicle*. He also wrote and illustrated five children's books, was a puppeteer, and painted murals in many Bay Area buildings, including the children's playrooms of the Stanford Convalescent Home (the old Stanford mansion) and at the old Palo Alto Medical Clinic. Wolo was born in Berlin and came to the United States as a Jewish refugee. He met Mrs. Lee, who helped resettle many refugees, and he boarded with the Lee family, living in the basement while doing some house projects in the summer of 1939.

The playroom mural depicted a long snake, mermaids carrying highball glasses filled with Champagne, a kangaroo with a zippered pouch containing billiard balls, three burping dilgahls (whatever they are), two hippos, and many other imaginative creatures, as well as the Lees' Welsh terrier, Ferdie. A portion of the mural was on wood, which the Lees took with them when they left the house, in 1955.

The house's landscaping also was notable, since Mrs. Lee was an avid gardener. With help two or three days a week from a fine Japanese gardener, George Kataguchi, she planted a large number and variety of flowers and shrubs, some of which remain, including a climbing rose that wanders through surrounding trees. The rock-lined driveway is surrounded by flower beds. Until Foothill Boulevard was constructed in the early 1930s, a double row of roses extended from the garden back to the foothills. The Lees planted a redwood tree for each of their children, and these trees are now a mature clump by the driveway entrance. However, the tree planted in the name of Margo died, almost an omen, since she did die early, in 1973.

One summer, while their parents were in Europe, the Lee sons—and a contractor who had never built a swimming pool—built a pool between two terrace walls in line with the living room. At times the boys would fill the pool by hose to bring warm water out from the house.

In 1938, based on two drawings by Birge Clark, the existing garage was turned into a library and an attached five-car garage was added. The 1,421-square-foot library had a lavatory in one corner, a fireplace in the opposite one, and numerous bookcases. The slightly larger new garage was set at an angle to the original one. Between the new spaces was a triangular room for tools and storage, with a door into the garage and another to the backyard.

Elsewhere on the property were three notable structures: a bowling alley, a foundry, and a playhouse. One summer, Dr. Lee, with some adult assistance and a little help from the boys, created the bowling alley in the service yard area below the kitchen—bordered by two lines of hollow concrete columns (of which five remain), each about 9 feet tall and perhaps 18 inches in diameter. The columns held plants and vines, to help improve the appearance of this playground in Dorothy Lee's eyes. Over the seasons, rain and shifting ground would cause the wooden alley to become rippled, so the boys had it resanded each year to reduce the slopes and slants. These idiosyncrasies gave the Lee family an advantage over visiting players who did not know the quirks. The boys and their friends rebuilt the bowling alley in the summer of 1939.

The second structure, in the extreme southern corner of the property, was a foundry shed about 20 by 36 feet for metal and other hobby work. Encouraged and led by their uncle Donald Lee, the boys made aluminum objects such as license frames. The structure's walls were made of concrete poured into corrugated-iron forms. This design was a Russel Lee original. The roof was corrugated metal, and a big door at one end could be lifted upward. At times the boys used the foundry to repair cars. In the mid-1990s, the building fell down and was removed.

The third structure was a playhouse, a wooden building with double doors and a shed roof that the boys made for their sister. Still standing, it can be used for "roughing it," while camping out in the backyard or for adventures by visiting grandchildren.

In addition to the family occupants, many students and other guests have lived in basement rooms or above the garage after the deck was converted to sleeping quarters in

In the living room, shape of arched alcove over fireplace repeats elsewhere in the house. The 11-foot ceiling has large beams across the room's width and crossbeams along its length.

Arched doorway under the staircase leads to loggia facing driveway.

the late 1930s. Students earned their keep by looking after the Lee children or working on the property. Also among the family was Leslie Langnecker (Luttgens), who lived with the Lees after her father, Dr. Harry Langnecker of Stanford's Medical School, died in 1936; the Langneckers had lived not far from the Lees, at 747 Santa Ynez. One occasional visitor was author Thomas Wolfe, who had met Dr. Lee on a ship returning to the U.S. from Germany in 1935. Another famous guest was Diego Rivera, while he was painting murals in the Coit Tower in San Francisco in the mid-1930s. John F. Kennedy visited one evening while he was briefly a Stanford student. An early student who worked for the Lees was said to have been a rumrunner during Prohibition.

The Owners

~Russel V. Lee~

Born in Utah in 1895, Russel Van Arsdale Lee attended Stanford for three years but graduated from the University of California in 1917 because he could do his first year of medical school and hold a job in the State Hygienic Laboratory. Lee's father had been a Presbyterian minister in Spanish Fork, Utah, later turning to beekeeping. After his father was disabled by an accident, the family moved to Berkeley, where his mother, at age 65, opened a successful boardinghouse.

After earning his M.D. degree from Stanford in 1918, Lee began an exceptionally long and illustrious career in the medical profession. He first joined the medical practice of internist Harold Hill in San Francisco. In 1918, he married Dorothy Lee Womach, a 1916 Stanford graduate. Four years later, the Lees moved with their three children to Palo Alto, where he joined Dr. Tom Williams. Their practice, at the corner of Hamilton Avenue and Bryant Street, soon grew to include Drs. Fritz Roth and Esther Clark, then Milton Saier and Blake Wilbur. In 1930, they founded the Palo Alto Medical Clinic, the first group practice on the West Coast. In addition to his practice, Lee served as executive director of the clinic and clinical professor of medicine at Stanford Medical School. From 1942 to 1945, Dr. Lee served in the Army Air Corps. His last assignment was as chief of preventive medicine for the Army Air Corps (later the Air Force). He also served on many university committees and as president of the Stanford Alumni Association, as well as on state and federal health advisory committees. In 1961, the PAMC dedicated its new Russel V. Lee Building. He retired from the clinic in 1960 at age 65 but continued as a consultant for another 15 years.

Second-floor view shows curved staircase with oak railings and balusters. Tendrils of wrought iron weave between them.

When the Lees moved into the house, in 1928, the family included daughter Margo and sons Richard Stanford, Peter, Philip, and Russel Hewlett (Hewey). All the children attended Stanford University and Stanford Medical School, and all would play prominent roles in medicine or public health. Richard, an obstetrician, practiced with the Palo Alto Medical Clinic (later the Palo Alto Medical Foundation) from 1952 to 1984; he died in 2003. Hewey Lee served for many years as clinical professor of surgery in the Stanford Medical School. He was the second of the next Lee generation to join the Palo Alto Medical Clinic (1956), and later served as its vice executive director (1964–80) and director (1980–90). Philip, an internist, also began his career at the clinic in 1956. In 1969, he joined the faculty of the University of California Medical School as professor of social medicine when he was appointed chancellor of the University of California at San Francisco. He has had a prominent career in public health, serving under Presidents Kennedy and Johnson, and most recently (1993–97) as assistant secretary for health in the Clinton administration. Peter joined the faculty of Stanford Medical School after completion of his residency training. He was soon recruited to USC, where he served for many years as a professor of medicine and the chairman of family medicine. Margo married Dr. James Paulson, a psychiatrist. Besides raising three children, she practiced family medicine, working principally for Planned Parenthood, while her husband practiced at the Palo Alto Medical Clinic and at Stanford Student Health Services, which was managed by the clinic.

In 1955, Russel and Dorothy Lee moved to 630 Los Trancos Road, Palo Alto, where they lived out their lives. Dorothy Lee died in 1972, her husband in 1982.

Between 1955 and 1958, Richard Lee and his wife, Louise, occupied the Gerona Road house until the senior Lees gave the house to the Stanford Medical School. During 1959 and into early 1960, the university rented the house to a Medical School clinical associate professor of psychiatry, Harry A. Wilmer, and his wife. After Stanford decided to sell the house, the Wilmers moved out, and an elderly couple named Anderson lived here for a short period, apparently as rent-free house sitters.

~John P. Bunker~

In 1960, the house was purchased by Dr. Bunker, a professor of anesthesia and of health research and policy at Stanford, and his wife, Mary. They and their four children lived there until 1965. Doctor Bunker's interests shifted more to health services research, and he remained on the faculty until he retired to the United Kingdom.

Dr. Bunker writes:

> 440 Gerona Road is a wonderful house...the University offered [it to me]. No price had been placed, however, and it was apparent that its availability had attracted little interest. There were, as I remember, broken windows, and it appeared somewhat shabby. I was nevertheless immediately attracted to it and began correspondence with the University Controller. The Controller suggested that I make an offer, and when I offered $32,000, it was immediately accepted. Russ Lee, I understand, was deeply upset that it had generated so small a sum....
>
> The house was in need of some immediate minor and moderate repairs, which we promptly undertook. I believe that the electrical wiring was the most important and serious problem needing attention. When major repairs were considered, I tended to defer them if no serious risks were involved. The advice was that if one component was strengthened, the water pipes perhaps, something else was sure to give way, the something else, already weakened, unable to withstand facing increased pressure.... I was reasonably successful in keeping the swimming pool functioning....

Mary Bunker provides the following:

> 440 Gerona is a beautifully designed house, aesthetically pleasing from every angle, with elegance, charm and luxury. Everyone enjoyed living or visiting there, unfortunately including insects and animals. When we arrived, termites had taken over the foundation and Rose's Pest Control crews became part of our family. Mice scurried through the attic and gophers dug trenches in the lawns....
>
> Our son had an extensive Lionel Train setup in the basement, and the girls used the playhouse for dolls and art projects. The pool gave everyone pleasure. One night two large Samoyeds from nearby jumped in, and it was a challenge to persuade them to leave. The gardens, especially the rose bushes, were a delight. My introduction to California flowers—the Canna lilies by the door to the pool—was unforgettable....

The house was too big even for a family with four children, so the Bunkers sold the property. "The girls

Under the ancient oak (shown on page 41), Dorothy Lee sits with her children: Phil, Dick, Margo, Peter, and Hewey.

Musical octet in 1945 includes Russel Lee and sons Richard, Phil, and Hewey in the back row; Peter, Dorothy Lee, and Margo in front. Dark-haired singer in the center is Leslie Langnecker, who lived with the Lees after the death of her father, Dr. Harry Langnecker.

have never forgiven us, as we dashed their dreams of wedding receptions with bouquets thrown down the front hall staircase."

~Robert J. Glaser~

In July 1965, Dr. Glaser and his wife, Dr. Helen Glaser, became the house's third owners. They bought it for about $56,000, a little more than twice the original construction cost, and sold it six years later for $89,000. The house served well for the Glasers and their three children.

Robert Glaser was professor of medicine, dean of the School of Medicine, and vice president for medical affairs. Before coming to Stanford in 1965, he had served on the medical school faculties of Harvard University, Washington University in St. Louis, and the University of Colorado. From September through November 1968, he also served briefly as acting president of Stanford, between Wallace Sterling's retirement and Kenneth Pitzer's arrival on December 1. Helen Glaser, who had been a practicing adult and child psychiatrist, died in 1999.

The largest alteration to the house was a complete remodeling of the kitchen and the breakfast area by George W. Reid Construction. The maid's room became a laundry room. Some of the electrical wiring had been done in a haphazard fashion, so considerable modernization was required to bring the power supply up to code. Parts of the house were painted. Since many of the original bronze casement window latches were missing, a local foundry recast replacements. Shelving was added in the study off the entry hall. The sleeping porch accommodated an extensive model train layout.

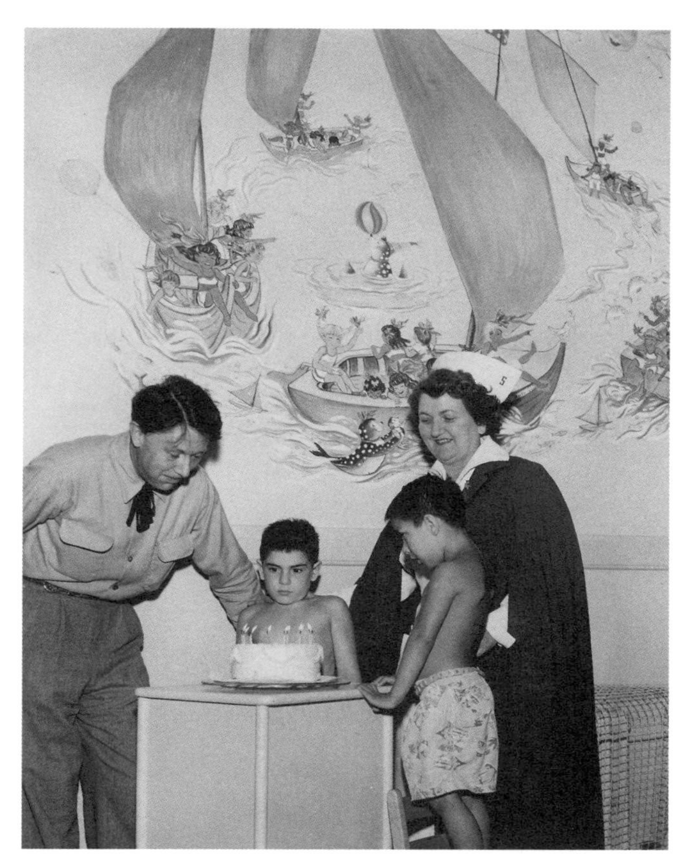

Artist-writer-puppeteer Wolo Trutzschler painted murals at Stanford Convalescent Home (above) as well as in the Lees' basement playroom.

During the era of campus protests in 1968, when Dr. Glaser was acting president, the university placed a red "hot line" telephone by his bed with direct connection to the Stanford Police Department. Dr. Glaser also had ultrasonic intrusion detection devices placed in the front and back halls. Fortunately, neither the hot line nor the devices had to be called into use.

In 1970, the Glasers moved to New York City, where Robert Glaser served as vice president of the Commonwealth Fund; he played an important part in the fund's support of the hospice movement in this country. Two years later, they returned to California when he became the first full-time president and chief executive officer of the Henry J. Kaiser Family Foundation, a post he held until 1983. From 1984 to 1997, he served as a trustee and director for medical science of the Lucille P. Markey Charitable Trust. Now a consulting professor of medicine, emeritus, at Stanford, Glaser remains active as a biomedical consultant and as a scientific adviser.

~William C. Dement~

Dement, a professor of psychiatry, and his wife, Pat, became the fifth owners in 1970, but the Glasers lived rent-free in the house during 1970–71 until they completed their move to New York City. At Stanford since 1963, Dement established the Stanford University Sleep Disorders Clinic in 1970. He started the publication *Sleep Reviews* and has written hundreds of scientific papers on sleep and dreaming.

In the early 1990s, the Dements added two things for their physically disabled daughter: a hot tub between the pool and the house, and a wooden ramp to the side entrance. They have also turned several rooms into studies or workrooms for scholarly projects. The Dements have entertained many large groups, using to their advantage the spaciousness of the house's interior and exterior. It has accommodated as many as 120 persons at sit-down dinners for special university occasions.

After some years of the garden's being allowed to

govern itself, the Dements have done wonders to rejuvenate it. Pat Dement grows vegetables behind the house and an extensive and luxurious spread of flowers in the large southeastern portion where Mrs. Lee also expressed her love of flowers. Today, daffodils, anemones, dahlias, roses, delphiniums, passion vines, and petunias bloom profusely in season. The wisteria-covered arbor over the brick garden terrace off the dining room is often favored by birds as a nesting place. Many weddings and Department of Athletics events, and a gala Stanford Elementary School class reunion have been held in the large backyard under the old valley oak tree. ❋

SOURCES

Board of Trustees, Stanford University. Supporting Documents, SC 27 (7 June 1926). Stanford University Archives.

Bunker, Mary. Letter to authors (20 August 1996).

Bunker, John P. Letter to authors (28 August 1996).

Clark, Birge, Alterations [drawings] (1935 and 1938). Birge Clark papers, Accession 96–105, File 408. Stanford University Archives.

Dement, Pat. House tour and interview with authors (15 July 1996).

"Dr. Robert J. Glaser Distinguished University Professorship Established." *Record* [Washington University in St. Louis] (18 January 2000).

Glaser, Helen. Interview with authors (1 August 1996).

Glaser, Robert J. Interview with authors (30 July 1996).

Junipero Serra Boulevard route [drawings], RD0042 and 0043. Stanford Maps and Records.

Lee, Philip. Verification of final copy for 440 Gerona (October 2004).

Lee, R. Hewlett. Interview with authors (13 August 1996).

Lee, Richard. Interview with authors (14 August 1996).

Lee, Russel V. [obit]. *New York Times* (29 January 1982).

Lee, Russel V. "The Good Old Days." *Stanford Magazine* 4, no. 2 (1976): 28–31.

Palo Alto Medical Foundation, "About PAMF: History of Innovation." Available at http://www.pamf.org/about/history/postwar.html

Trutzschler von Falkenstein, Baron Wolff Erhardt Anton Georg (Wolo) [obit]. *San Francisco Chronicle* (5 October 1989).

PHOTOS

Lee family and 1945 house exterior, Hewlett Lee collection; Wolo, *Palo Alto Times*/Susan Christiansen collection; all others, Margaret McKinnon.

536 Gerona Road

BYRON FEIG

1929 ~ Tudor period style

ARCHITECT
Charles K. Sumner

OWNERS
Craig—Goheen—Jackson
—Robbins

BY KATHY CUSICK AND DEBBY ROBBINS

This Tudor period house, designed for Hardin Craig, has typical elements of this architectural style: steeply pitched roofs and gables as well as tall windows with small panes. But rather than one façade facing the street, the stucco house comprises three separate units, slightly offset from each other. These units abut a larger back section running perpendicular to them; continuing from this section is the living room, two steps lower than the main house. All in all, the house has a comfortable look to it, as if units had been added as the family grew, a practice not uncommon in English houses. And in the spring of 2005, additions faithful to the original style are under way.

The original construction, by Edward J. Schmaling, cost about $14,500 and was completed in mid-September 1929.

From the driveway, a walk along the right side of the garage leads to the front door. Inside is an entry hall, about 6 by 15 feet, with the living room to the right. The main floor also comprises the dining room, kitchen, master bedroom and bath, a small study, laundry room, and maid's room and bath.

Though not noticeable from the street, the living room lies at a slight angle from the main house. At both ends of the room are built-in bookshelves, with a window between the ones on the far wall. A fireplace in the middle of the long side wall has a molded-concrete mantel and surround, now stained dark; to the left of the fireplace, a windowed door in an alcove opens onto a small brick terrace with steps down into the garden. The louvered window treatment in this room allows in much light without harsh sun; in fact, the whole house has a very light and warm feeling.

In the study is a small fireplace edged with small rectangular tiles patterned with vines and leaves against a blue background. The mantel is almost classical in its simplicity. The doorways in the main downstairs rooms have round lintels that echo the round-arched front entrance.

The living room's brass light sconces are original, as are the dining room chandelier, the entrance hall light in a brass hoop, and fixtures in the study and maid's room. In the mid-'90s, the Jackson family, brief owners, had the fixtures cleaned and restored to their original brightness. Elsewhere, ceiling fixtures have been replaced by ones in keeping with the original style.

Several rooms, including the front hall and living room, have sponge-painted treatments to enhance architectural details and provide a warmer look than a flat coat of paint would (the hall's arched ceiling is painted sky blue).

In 2000, the kitchen was updated. The wall between the kitchen and pantry was removed, the ceiling was replaced, and recessed lighting and a tile floor with mosaic inlay were added. The cabinets were painted sage green and have new pewter hardware. The kitchen and laundry room were also painted, and molding was added to recapture the house's original look, which had been diminished by an earlier remodel, probably in the 1950s. (For details on renovations in progress during 2005, see page 51.)

According to the blueprints, the 6- by 10-foot pantry was intended to be a breakfast nook. (As for all the rooms, the blueprints show faint lines of prospective furniture placement.)

The maid's bath has doors to the bedroom and laundry room, which opens to the garage and also onto a small walled service yard.

Upstairs are two bedrooms with a bath between them, a linen closet in the hallway at the head of the stairs, and an attic over the kitchen.

The basement, about 9 by 10 feet, contains the hot-water tank, furnace, and heating pipes; stairs under the main

Brick walkway to front of house is lined with vinca.
In 2005, new construction blends with old: bay window replaces garage door; interior will be a family room.

staircase in the entrance hall lead down to it. The good-sized attic room, though unfinished and still with the original knob-and-tube wiring, offers ample storage space as the original blueprints indicated; its window looks out over the garage roof onto the street.

The Owners

~Hardin Craig~

The house's first owner was Hardin Craig, professor of English, who came to Stanford in 1928. Craig initially lived in Palo Alto but moved with his family to 536 Gerona soon after it was finished, in September 1929.

Craig was born in 1875 on a farm near Owensboro, Kentucky. He received his A.B. in 1897 from Centre College in Kentucky and his M.A. (1899) and Ph.D. (1901) in English literature from Princeton. Before coming to Stanford, he taught at Princeton and the University of Minnesota, and was the head of the Department of English at the University of Iowa. When he retired from teaching at Stanford at the end of spring quarter 1939, he was chairman of the Council of the School of Letters, which included religion, classics, English, and Romance and Slavic languages. He continued to teach: until 1949 at the University of North Carolina, then until 1960 at the University of Missouri. He died in Houston in 1968.

He was a well-known Shakespeare scholar and editor, and for several years before the fall of 1940, he was a research associate at the Henry E. Huntington Library and Art Gallery in San Marino.

~Interim Occupants~

From 1940 through mid-1945, the house was occupied by Charles Albro Barker, assistant professor of history. Barker, born in Washington in 1904, had received his A.B. in 1926 and his Ph.D. in history in 1932 from Yale. That year, he married Louise Chase Cottle in Northampton, Massachusetts. He taught at Stanford from 1933 to 1945, then left in the summer of 1947 to be professor and head of the Department of History at Johns Hopkins University. His biography of Henry George, the economist, was "highly acclaimed," and he was an early member of the peace movement. He died in Santa Barbara in 1993.

Hardin Craig

Neal E. Van Sooy, who had received his A.B. in journalism in 1933 from Stanford, lived in the house for about two years. Before his appointment as alumni director in the fall of 1943, he had owned the *Azusa Herald*, was general manager of the *Redwood City Daily Tribune*, and served as a full-time lecturer in Stanford's Division of Journalism. He moved into the Gerona Road house in autumn 1945 but resigned from Stanford in May 1947 to resume his career in newspaper publishing, having bought the *Santa Paula Daily Chronicle* in Ventura County. He died in 1990.

Another brief occupant was Clarence H. Faust, who came to Stanford in 1947 as director of university libraries and professor of English. He received his B.A. from North Central College, B.D. from Evangelical Theological Seminary, and M.A. and Ph.D. in English from the University of Chicago. Faust was on the Chicago faculty for 17 years in various positions, including dean of students in the Division of Humanities, professor of English and dean of the college, and dean of the Graduate Library School.

In the front hallway, original hoop light casts interesting shadows. Through the arch, living room extends at a slight angle.

In September 1948, Alvin Eurich, Stanford's acting president after the death of Donald Tresidder, appointed Faust dean of Stanford's newly formed School of Humanities and Sciences. Soon after, when Eurich decided to leave Stanford to head New York's reorganization of its state universities, Faust was named Stanford's acting president until the arrival of J. E. Wallace Sterling in April 1949. Faust then resumed his position as dean of the School of Humanities and Sciences. In mid-March 1951, he left Stanford for the presidency of the Ford Foundation's Fund for the Advancement of Education. He died in Los Angeles in 1975.

~John David Goheen~

The next owner was John Goheen, professor of philosophy at Stanford from 1951 until 1972 and university ombudsman from 1974 to 1985. Goheen, born in 1906, received his A.B. in philosophy from Pomona College in 1929 and M.A. a year later from Claremont College. After three years at the Sorbonne, he returned to this country to earn his Ph.D. from Harvard in 1935.

John Goheen

Subsequently, he taught at Harvard, Wellesley, and Queen's College Long Island. In 1950, President Sterling recruited him to be executive head of Stanford's Philosophy Department. In the 1950s and '60s, Goheen played a key role in setting up Stanford's programs in Japan. He also helped develop the Structured Liberal Education program and was director of freshman seminars. Goheen continued to teach after his retirement, and in 1974 took on the responsibilities of university ombudsman (he preferred *ombudsperson*). A popular professor, he was very effective in that position. His wife, Nancy Reid Goheen, died in the late 1970s. He died in 1994, while still residing in his house.

~Michael Jackson~

Again the house was only briefly occupied when Michael Jackson bought it from the Goheen estate in July 1994. He received an A.B. in anthropology from Stanford in 1972, and M.Ed. (1974) and Ed.D. (1976) from the University of Massachusetts, Amherst. From 1980, Jackson served various positions at Stanford, the last as dean of students from 1991 to 1995. He left to be vice president of student affairs at the University of Southern California.

Living room alcove opens to the back garden.

Dark finish on molded-concrete fireplace gives it the look of mahogany or other dark wood.

From 1988 to 1995, his wife, Diana D. Akiyama, served as associate and acting dean of Memorial Church.

Though the family lived in the house for only four months, during that time they retiled the upstairs bath and updated the maid's room bath. They also refinished the mahogany floors. The biggest change they made, however, was in the garden: clearing out overgrowth, pulling ivy off the house, and repainting the house. All this created a more open look to the garden and made the house stand out.

~Robert Robbins~

The current owner is a cardiac surgeon at Stanford Medical School who came to Stanford in 1993. Robbins was born in Laurel, Mississippi; he received his B.S. in chemistry from Millsaps College and his M.D. from the University of Mississippi. He trained in cardiothoracic surgery at Stanford, Emory University, and the Royal Victoria Children's Hospital in Melbourne, Australia. Robert and Debby Robbins, with their two young sons, moved into the house in March 1995.

The front garden and front door are visible from the street, the lawn edged by a low stone wall that separates it from ivy, flowering vinca, and roses growing by the street.

The garden was relandscaped in 2000 with a new lawn and sprinkler system, and extensive plantings including roses, lilies, hydrangeas, lavender, and citrus. The garden blooms almost year-round and is true to the house's age and architectural style. Lawn areas on the side and back of the house slope down to a stone sitting area; it has an original stone bench and a column with white 'Iceberg' roses spilling over the top, and is surrounded by white roses and 'Johnson's Blue' geraniums. Against the steps from the living room to the brick patio grows a pink-touched white rose, probably growing there since the house was built. The level side yard next to the kitchen extends to a low stone wall and an upper level planted with herbs and flowers including daffodils, gaura, and lilies. A magnificent oak tree shades a crushed granite sitting area. Beyond the back lawn area, the periphery of the back garden has been left in its natural state with many trees, blackberry bushes, and calla lilies giving it a wild look.

In early 2005, new construction is under way, designed by Bill Bocook, AIA, and built by contractor Bill Stich. It is carefully crafted to tie in with Charles Sumner's original design, including stucco exterior, similar roof slopes and shingling, and multipaned windows. A new driveway on the left of the house runs back to a two-car garage with an upper story for storage; its decorative cupola matches one on the former garage, which will become a family room with a bay window facing the street. The kitchen has been pushed out toward the new driveway to form a breakfast nook and mudroom, but the sitting area under the oak will remain. The second-floor attic will become a study for the Robbinses' sons. ❋

Former sitting area under old oak, now inundated with debris, will be reclaimed once construction ends.

SOURCES

Akiyama, Diana, http://www.oxy.edu/articles/030711-akiyama.html

Barker, Charles A. [obit]. *Washington Post* (16 September 1993): B6.

Blueprints, 1929. In possession of Robert Robbins (2003).

"Charles Ambro Barker and Louise Chase Cottle" [marriage]. (24 July 1932).

"Charles K. Sumner" [obit]. *Palo Alto Times* (26 May 1948): 1.

"Clarence Faust appointed Director of Libraries October 1947, acting president 1 January–30 March 1949." Paul C. Edwards to Wallace Sterling, 6 December 1948. Stanford University Archives card file (no citation), SC170/2/6. Cited in Gillmor, C. Stewart. *Fred Terman: Building a Discipline, a University, and Silicon Valley.* Stanford University Press (2004).

"Dean Faust Is Acting President." Local history file, Stanford Archives (ca. 1949).

"Dean Faust's resignation accepted 'with regret.'" *Stanford Alumni Review* 52, no. 7 (March 1951): 12.

Faust, Clarence H. [death announcement; news release], Stanford University News Service (21 May 1975).

Goheen, John David [appointment; news release]. Director of Information, Stanford University News (3 May 1950).

"Hardin Craig, Teacher, Is Dead; Shakespeare Scholar and Editor" [obit]. *The New York Times* (16 October [dateline] 1968).

Jackson, Michael. http://www.usc.edu/admin/provost/bios/jackson.html

Maxwell, Baldwin, et al (eds.). *Renaissance Studies in Honor of Hardin Craig*. Stanford University Press (1941).

"Neal Edgar Van Sooy" [obit]. *Peninsula Times Tribune* (21 Feb 1990).

"New Library Director" [Clarence H. Faust]. *Stanford Alumni Review* 49, no. 17 (October 1947): 17.

"Ombudsman Goheen: Master of Diplomacy." *Stanford Daily* (1 May 1980): 5.

"Philosophy professor and ombudsperson emeritus Goheen dies at 87" [news release]. Stanford News Service (30 March 1994).

"President of Fund Is Ending Service: Clarence Faust Is Retiring from Educational Group." *The New York Times* (20 March 1966).

"Retiring Professor Says No One Way to Teach" [John Goheen]. *Campus Report* 4, no. 24 (5 April 1972): 8.

Stokes, Donald. "Lightning Rod for 'Human Stories' to Step Down as Ombudsperson" [John Goheen]. *Campus Report* 17, no. 36 (12 June 1985): 5–6.

"Van Sooy, N." *Stanford Alumni Review* 45, no. 1 (October 1943): 4.

"Van Sooy Resigns: Alumni Director to re-enter newspaper publishing." *Stanford Alumni Review* 48, no. 9 (June 1947): 7.

PHOTOS

Craig, Stanford News Service; Goheen, Stanford Archives; all others, Margaret McKinnon.

Gables, varying roof lines, and the sloping lot minimize the mass of the house, giving it a cottage look. Large trees provide privacy.

548 Gerona Road

BYRON FEIG

1928 ~ Tudor period style

ARCHITECT	OWNERS
Birge M. Clark	Stuart—Wilbur—Spurr/Heckler

BY MARIAN LEIB ADAMS

This charming house that architect Birge Clark designed in 1928 for his friends Graham and Agnes Stuart defies easy categorization. Though its basic style is Tudor, it might best be described as picturesque with elements of simplified Gothic revival and medieval English cottage. The house—which was built for $24,000—has an asymmetric design, with gabled roofs of different heights, windows of different shapes and styles, and interesting decorative elements.

Like many of Birge Clark's houses, this one is eclectic, and its charm is in its layout, its craftsmanship, and its detailing. In the original house plan, two squirrels are drawn on the western elevation of the lot, revealing the playfulness of both draftsman and designer.

Though it's a large house (3,668 square feet), it's cozy, with touches of the Brothers Grimm. The west-facing front door, under a gable and a Gothic arch, has its original medieval-looking grille and lantern. The arch design repeats in the shape of the 4-inch-thick door, in a ventilation grille above the door, in several interior passageways, and in the living room fireplace. (Imaginative venting designs are one hallmark of Birge Clark's architecture.) To the right of the front door is a larger gable over an elegant living room window framed by narrow, vertical glass panes and topped with a multipaned glass strip and a redwood lintel. Above the gable window, another louvered vent projects from the wall on brackets and suggests a tower room, perhaps for a tiny Rapunzel.

With so many details to see in this house, the roof's wonderful mix of shapes, angles, curves, and levels might initially be overlooked. The cedar-shingle roof is primarily steeply pitched. The ridgeline curves up so slightly as to be almost undetectable. Gables on every side of the house connect to the main roof in curved or straight lines, no two roofs exactly alike. Most remarkable is the gable over the front door, where the roofline runs straight to a larger gable on the right, and runs curved to the main roof on the left. There are three chimneys, one each to the fireplaces in the living room and the study, and one to ventilate the kitchen.

Numerous multipaned windows and small arched windows on the north and south sides of the house continue the charming irregularities in window shapes, sizes, and placement. French doors on the west and south sides open onto patios and gardens, catching fine views.

An elaborate landscape plan, designed for the Stuarts by Gardner A. Dailey, of San Francisco, included many old oak trees; three 200-year-old valley oaks *(Quercus lobata)* remain. The plan also included a rose garden, a field of native plants and shrubs to the south, a lilac walkway, a fruit tree walkway, and a vista-lawn on the west side of the house. Most of these original plantings are gone, except for the rose garden and many of the shrubs.

The house has an enormous attic. Supposedly, Birge Clark wanted to build a two-story house, but Mrs. Stuart was equally convinced that she wanted a single-level home. From the size of the attic, it seems that they both got what they wanted.

Living room fireplace is painted stucco with an exposed-brick hearth. The firebox's arch is similar to the shapes of the heavy redwood front door and interior doorway, which have identical Tudor-inspired outlines. Note inside door's thickness.

A footpath from the street leads to the house's front entrance through a *torii*, a Japanese gate that was added later. To the right of the entrance is the 19- by 30-foot living room and to the left is a wing of three bedrooms, a sleeping porch, and two bathrooms. The floors and millwork in the living areas are American white oak, with pine floors in what were the servants' quarters. The exterior millwork is redwood, as are the window frames and the half-timbers over the larger windows. The exterior walls are pigmented stucco, while the interior ones are lath and plaster.

The living room boasts a 14-foot ceiling of tongue-and-groove redwood with hand-hewn beams. The room's centerpiece is the fireplace: painted stucco over brick with a plaster hood and shelf, and a brick hearth. A large picture window, between two French doors, looks onto a sheltered patio.

In the bedroom wing, the sleeping porch was closed off by adding an inside door to make a fourth bedroom.

The kitchen is at the end of the hall between the bedroom wing and the living room. Its original built-in cabinets have been refaced, but the original cold cupboard is intact and functioning. From the kitchen, a door opens onto the sunroom and another door, to its right, to the dining room. The sunroom has one door to the service porch, and a second door onto a patio framed by the study and sunroom. The dining room opens to the living room and the study. Outdoors, the living room and study walls form a corner patio that is accessible through French doors on each side of the 4- by 6 1/2-foot living room window.

Reached from the sunroom are the service porch and an apartment comprising the original servant's room and garage. Stairs from the service porch lead to the half basement, which is now a workshop. Outside a sunroom adjoining the service porch and dining room is a second patio. A third patio is bordered by the bedroom wing, the kitchen and service porch, and the garage.

Owners and Occupants

~Graham Stuart~

Stuart, who was born in Cleveland in 1886, was a multifaceted man who earned his way through college by playing the nickelodeon for silent movies. In 1908, he earned his bachelor's degree from Western Reserve University. Although his early ambition was to be a foreign correspondent, he became interested in the foreign service and then studied at the École Libre des Sciences Politiques in Paris.

In 1918, he received his Ph.D. from the University of Wisconsin and taught there until 1923, when he came to Stanford as the university's first international relations specialist. He wrote several books on foreign relations and is probably best known for his work on Latin America and the United States.

As much a teacher as a scholar, Stuart inspired many of his students to enter the diplomatic corps, and several became ambassadors for the United States. During World War II, he served in Washington, D.C., as chief economic analyst on the Board of Economic Warfare, and in 1948 he was appointed to the Advisory Committee of the Foreign Service Institute.

Professor Stuart retired from Stanford in 1952. In 1978, the Board of Trustees established an endowed professorship in his name. Stuart is also credited with launching the annual Stanford Alumni Conference, which grew from a casual conversation with a group of former students to a format that now sends faculty members all over the world to reconnect with alumni through Alumni Association and Development Office events.

Graham Stuart and his wife, Agnes Wright Stuart, were married for 65 years. They met when he was teaching at Glenville High School near Cleveland. Agnes's younger sister was a student of Stuart's and invited him home to

ELENA ANGOLOTI

View of north side of house shows its characteristic series of gables and irregularly spaced small-paned windows.

Graham Stuart

meet her family. Agnes, who graduated with honors from Vassar, wanted to be a doctor and had been accepted to medical school, but her father would not pay her tuition because he felt medical school would be too much for her health. Being a young woman in the early 20th century, Agnes could not qualify for a student loan by herself. Undaunted, she chose social work as a career.

The Stuarts had two daughters, Ann Stuart Orloff and Jean Stuart Frost, and eight grandchildren. Ann Orloff and three of her daughters are physicians, undoubtedly encouraged by Mrs. Stuart. Ann remembers her as a dedicated gardener and bird enthusiast, and someone who enjoyed welcoming newcomers to the campus. She also remembers driving the family car about the campus when she was only 9, doing errands for the family.

It is ironic that Agnes's desire for a one-story house brought 548 Gerona Road to the attention of Ray Lyman Wilbur and his wife, Marguerite Blake Wilbur. When they left the presidential home on the Knoll, she was in a wheelchair (the result of a riding accident) and required a single-story house. The university persuaded the Stuarts to sell the house, one of the few single-story ones on campus, and in 1942 they moved to 450 Santa Rita Avenue in Palo Alto. The Wilburs moved to Gerona Road in June 1943.

Graham Stuart died in 1983.

~RAY LYMAN WILBUR~

Wilbur, who was president of Stanford from 1916 to 1942, was born in 1875 in Boone, Iowa. From there his family moved to the Dakota Territory, and later to Riverside, California. A member of Stanford's 1896 graduating class, he helped pay for his education by working as a laboratory assistant in his major department of physiology. A fellow Encina Hall resident, Herbert Hoover, was to become a lifelong friend.

Wilbur received a master's degree in 1897 and his medical degree in 1899 from the Cooper Medical College in San Francisco, which in 1908 became the Stanford Medical School. After graduate work in Europe, he became an assistant professor in 1900. Following a few years of private practice in Palo Alto, he became a professor of medicine in 1909, and then dean of the Stanford Medical School in 1911. He accepted the presidency of Stanford in 1916 at 40 years of age. In the following 30 years, he reached eminence in three fields: higher education, public service, and medical science.

During Dr. Wilbur's 25 years as president, he encouraged several new developments that shaped the modern university: the adoption of the quarter system to allow the university to be open year-round; self-government by the students, with the adoption of a successful honor code to govern exams and social conduct; a plan for independent study for exceptional students; the grouping of related departments into schools so that students could move freely among fields of interest; the launching of a School of Humanities with the scope of a liberal arts college; and the lifting of the limit of 500 women at the university.

Slight curves on roof's edges add to house's fairy-tale look.

Wilbur took a four-year leave of absence during his presidency to serve as U.S. secretary of the interior under President Herbert Hoover and turned the attention of the department to conservation. He also served as president of the American Medical Association in 1923–24, after which he continued to exert considerable influence in medicine as chairman of the Council on Medical Education and Hospitals.

In 1898, while still a medical student, Wilbur married Marguerite May Blake, who was born in 1875 in San Francisco. She was a premedical student at Stanford, and they met in 1895 in a summer program at Hopkins Marine Station in Pacific Grove. She received an A.B. degree in physiology in 1897 but gave up her career when she married. Mrs. Wilbur was an active volunteer, including serving on the board of the Stanford Convalescent Home (later Children's Hospital at Stanford) and doing Belgian relief work during World War I. The Wilburs had five children. Much of Mrs. Wilbur's life is chronicled in her journal, "Doings," which she maintained for her children. It also records much of the remodeling at 548 Gerona Road during their ownership.

The Wilburs were able to work with the original architect, Birge Clark, to make a few changes to accommodate their special needs, while keeping intact the house's architectural integrity.

Widening the doorways in the bedroom wing allowed wheelchair access. The garage was converted into two rooms for the servants, and a carport was built with a covered walkway to the house. The laundry room was converted to a dining and sitting room for the servants, and the laundry area moved to the basement. Ceramic tile floors were added to one bathroom, and some plumbing and electrical improvements were done. Work progressed slowly, however, because materials and labor were rationed during World War II. But by summer 1943, the Wilburs could move to their new home. Mrs. Wilbur's journal notes that on September 2, 1943, she held her first "Thursday at home" and entertained 25 ladies. In 1944, the Wilburs added a small toolshed next to the garage.

Mrs. Wilbur, shown in a painted photograph, took great joy in the garden, bringing plants from their former home in Palo Alto to grow in the Gerona garden.

Stanford's second president, Ray Lyman Wilbur, is shown in a photograph probably taken in the 1920s.

Mrs. Wilbur loved flowers, and she supervised many changes in the garden. She searched the Peninsula for plants that she liked, and she transplanted begonias, camellias, and hellebores from their original Palo Alto home at 1201 Bryant to the president's house at Stanford, and finally to 548 Gerona. She writes of the special joy of a first-year garden when plants sprout and bloom for the first time. Her oldest granddaughter, Jessica Ely Hart, remembers learning to arrange flowers under her grandmother's tutelage, and that Mrs. Wilbur's favorite color in the house and in the garden was blue.

Christmas was a special time for the family, especially for Mrs. Wilbur, who was very artistic and a perfectionist, and who loved the preparations for the holidays. Jessica Hart remembers being taught to wrap Christmas presents with red and green tissue paper and ribbons curled at the ends.

Dr. Wilbur, known to some of his grandchildren as "John-daddy," was a wise and warm presence in the life of his grandson, Leonard Ely, who remembers learning to fish in the summers at the family compound, The Cedars, near Soda Springs in the Sierra. He also remembers that life at 548 Gerona Road was quiet, as both of his grandparents had physical problems, and his mother, Jessica Wilbur Ely, basically ran the house for them.

Mrs. Wilbur died in December 1946, and Dr. Wilbur lived in the house until his death, in June 1949.

~WILLIAM SPURR~

Spurr, a specialist in business statistics in the Graduate School of Business, bought the house from the university in 1949 and moved there with his wife, Hallie Rucker Spurr, and their two daughters. They later had two sons, and raised all four children in the house.

Spurr was born in 1905 in Washington, D.C., and was raised in New York state. His father, Josiah Edward Spurr, was an eminent geologist; a mineral and an active volcano in Alaska were named for him. At age 19, William Spurr graduated, magna cum laude, from Harvard in mathematics and astronomy. He spent a year as a naval aviator on a Harvard expedition to view a solar eclipse in Sumatra, then he earned his M.B.A. at Harvard in 1928. After some years in the business world, he entered Columbia University, where he received his Ph.D. in 1940. In 1937, he had begun teaching at the University of Nebraska. During World War II, he was an economist in Washington, D.C., returning to the Navy in 1942. Before coming to Stanford in 1946, he was at the University of Chicago. Professor Spurr died in Hawaii in 1975.

His widow, Hallie, continued to live in the house, and in 1981 she married Herb Heckler, a retired electrical engineer. They share a love of sailing and met at the Palo Alto Yacht Club.

During the Spurr-Heckler residency, the house has undergone several renovations, but always with the intent of preserving its architectural integrity. The Wilburs' carport was walled in to become a garage, and in 1978 the cedar-shingle roof was replaced. The driveway was expanded into a horseshoe shape with two entrances from Gerona Road. In the study, French doors have been converted to a picture window, and the west wall has freestanding shelves. The 1989 Loma Prieta earthquake damaged the chimney in the study, and it was rebuilt with schist and stucco. The dining room now serves as a library, with a built-in wall of bookshelves and a dictionary stand.

Edward Spurr, Hallie Heckler's son, helped landscape the property and built two *torii*, one at the entrance to the house, and the other, which was converted from the children's swing, off the sunroom. The Hecklers have recently added a covered swimming pool visible from Gerona Road Hallie Heckler, an avid rockhound, uses the toolshed to house her lapidary equipment and rock specimens. ❋

Hand-hewn beams support a tongue-and-groove redwood ceiling; multipaned window faces the front of the house.

SOURCES

Clark, Birge. Original house plans. Collection of Hallie Spurr Heckler.

Dailey, Gardner A. Landscape plans. Collection of Hallie Spurr Heckler.

Ely, Leonard W., Jr. Interview with author (19 June 2003).

Endowed Professorships & Directorships at Stanford University. Board of Trustees of Stanford University (1992): 265.

"Graham Stuart, 97, Dies after Surgery." *Campus Report* (4 May 1983).

Hart, Jessica Ely. Conversation with author (7 May 2003).

Heckler, Hallie Spurr. Interviews with author (fall 2002 and spring 2003).

Memorial Resolution: Graham Stuart (1886–1983). Stanford University Academic Council.

Orloff, Ann Stuart. Interview with author (2 June 2003).

"Poli Sci professor dies at 97." *Stanford Daily* (4 May 1983).

Program, 1941: the 25th anniversary of the presidency of Ray Lyman Wilbur. Bio files, Stanford Archives.

"Ray Lyman Wilbur" [obit]. *Palo Alto Times* (27 June 1949).

"Ray Lyman Wilbur, '96, Retiring from Presidency after 27 years." *Stanford Alumni Review* 44, no. 10 (July 1943): 3–17.

Stuart, Graham. Biographical summary. Bio files, Stanford Archives.

Swain, Robert, "Ray Lyman Wilbur: 1875–1949." *Science* 3, no. 2883 (31 March 1950): 324–327.

Turner, Paul V., Wattis Professor of Art at Stanford. Exterior house tour with author (April 2003).

Wilbur, Marguerite Blake. "Doings" [letters to her children]. (January 1942–May 1944).

"William Spurr" [death; news release]. Stanford News Service (11 March 1975).

PHOTOS

Stuart, Stanford News Service; Ray Lyman Wilbur and Marguerite Wilbur, Stanford Archives; all others, Leni Hazlett and Marian Adams.

593 Gerona Road

BYRON FEIG

1926 ~ Tudor period style

ARCHITECT
Charles K. Sumner

OWNERS
Mears—Gibson

By Therese L. Baker-Degler

In the 1920s, Gerona Road was at the outer edge of the campus area that was being developed for faculty residences. One of the first houses on the street was built in 1926 by Eliot Grinnell Mears and his wife, Gladys Chute Mears. Since then it has remained one of the few campus houses to be owned by descendants of the original family, in this case the Mearses' eldest daughter, Helen Gibson. In 1960, ownership passed to her and her husband, Weldon (Hoot) Gibson.

The house's Tudor period design is characteristic of Charles Sumner's work in other campus houses, including 421, 445, and 450 El Escarpado, though half-timbering on this house is on the back rather than on the front façade. Contractor was Wells P. Goodenough; total construction cost about $23,600.

With its irregularity and variety of detail, the house is a fine example of this architectural style. It has a vaguely medieval "storybook" form, with a segmental stone arch surrounding the recessed front doorway. The chimney pots and steeply pitched gabled roof are also typical Sumner details.

The architect's written specifications detail both choices of materials and expectations for the workers' performance. For example, he indicated that the front steps and terrace walls should be built from rubble and stones of campus buildings that had been demolished by the 1906 earthquake: "Stone shall be provided and delivered by the Owner from old buildings on the Stanford campus." Some of these stones, from the damaged Memorial Church, had fragments of mosaic tiles embedded in them. (Nearly 80 years later, these mosaic chips can still be seen in some stones near the front entrance.)

On his expectations for the quality of work to be done and the centrality of his control over the work being carried out, Sumner wrote: "Workmanship: The contractor shall discharge any employee who, in the opinion of the Architect, is objectionable or incompetent."

Sumner also pointed out features of the house in which he will be specifically involved: "[The living room fireplace]...mantel shall be stone complete as shown ready for setting, to be made where directed by the Architect. Allow the sum of $250.00 f.o.b. San Francisco for this material."

Or referring to specific features of the house, he wrote: "Stairs are to be guaranteed noiseless." "Provide buzzer in kitchen to ring from floor push in dining room."

The front entrance opens onto a generous entry hall with a coffered ceiling. To the left is the 17- by 24-foot living room with a stone fireplace, and to the right is the 14- by 19-foot dining room. Behind the dining room, the kitchen still has many features typical of the 1920s, such as a cool closet and an ironing board cupboard.

Up from the entry hall, a staircase landing has a tall arched window whose frame alludes to the segmented detail around the front door. From an arched door on the landing, a back staircase leads down to what was once the housekeeper's room.

On the second floor, the original plan contained two bedrooms, a master bedroom with a large sleeping porch, which was used as a fourth bedroom, a study on the front of the house, and a deck over the garage. In 1935, Charles Sumner replaced part of the deck with a fifth bedroom with shower and toilet; a small deck area remained. This bedroom had a separate entrance, reached by stairs from the garden.

When the house was built, the surrounding area was open land with only a few trees (see photo on page 64). This gave the Mears family free rein in developing their garden. The first landscaping included a formal rose garden on the right side of the house and a "summer house" with a palm-thatched roof at the back.

The architect also made changes to the landscaping. The gardens were terraced, the rose garden was replaced with a lawn and the fish pond with a fountain, and

On landing, tall window has segmented arch of painted wood blocks and a window seat below. Door at right opens to back staircase.

wisteria—still blooming after 70 years—was planted on a new arbor. Four redwood trees, 6 feet tall when they were planted next to the driveway, are now giants.

In 1960, after the Gibsons moved into the house, architect Mogens Mogensen replaced a shaded patio at the back of the house with a 20- by 23-foot family room. It still accommodates the extended family, who continue Gladys Mears's traditional Thanksgiving dinners. Currently, Helen Gibson uses it as a studio for her watercolor painting.

In 2000, civil engineer Steven Arnold upgraded the garage-top apartment by adding a sitting room. At the same time, a breakfast room next to the family room was converted to a bathroom to make an accessible living space for Hoot Gibson.

Helen Gibson notes how well the house has withstood its 79 years. The original shingle roof has had to be replaced only twice. No significant damage occurred to the house in the 1989 Loma Prieta earthquake.

Family treasures at the house include American antique furniture, mostly from Eliot Mears's family in Massachusetts, a collection of dolls from around the world assembled by Gladys Mears and added to by Helen Gibson, a letter to Gladys Mears from Mrs. Herbert Hoover, and a note from Winston Churchill to Hoot Gibson. Also notable are many of Helen Gibson's watercolor paintings; one of the house appeared on the Gibsons' 1967 Christmas card (see page 64) and again in her husband's book on the founding of Stanford Research Institute (SRI).

Owners and Occupants

~Eliot Grinnell Mears~

Mears came to Stanford in 1921 as a member of the Economics Department. In 1925, he joined the developing Graduate School of Business as a professor of geography and international trade.

He was born in 1889 in Worcester, Massachusetts, to the Reverend David Otis Mears and Mary Grinnell Mears, an early organizer of the National Parent-Teachers Association. His maternal grandfather, Josiah Bushnell Grinnell, founded the town of Grinnell, Iowa. After receiving his bachelor's degree from Harvard in 1910, Eliot Mears earned his M.B.A. from the Harvard Graduate School of Business and remained at the school as its secretary. In 1914, he married Gladys Chute, who had "gone West" from Massachusetts to study music at Oberlin College.

In 1916, Mears entered the U.S. Bureau of Foreign and Domestic Commerce, where he served as chief of the Foreign Service Division. This was the beginning of his extensive international experience. Later, Mears's international work continued to take him throughout Europe, the Middle East, and South America. He played an important role in the Institute of Pacific Relations, which was both a fact-finding body under the leadership of Ray Lyman Wilbur that produced *A Survey of Race Relations* and an organization promoting international contact through conferences. At a conference in Honolulu in 1925, Mears noted the reduction of prejudice against "Orientals," and supported the protests of the Japanese against discriminatory U.S. immigration legislation.

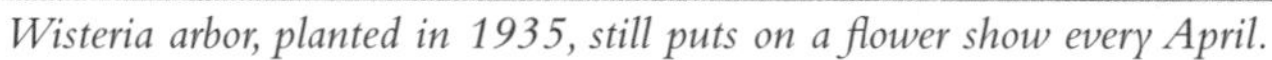

Wisteria arbor, planted in 1935, still puts on a flower show every April.

Eliot Grinnell Mears

At Stanford, Eliot Mears helped found the Graduate School of Business. He also served as the director of Stanford's summer sessions from 1932 until 1943, a role in which he fostered international contacts and programs as ways for the university to extend its influence on the world community.

In the late 1930s, the house was the site of several meetings to discuss the formation of a Stanford research institute. Hoot Gibson, in his history of SRI, remembers, as a graduate student living in the house, sitting in on several sessions where Herbert Hoover, Ray Lyman Wilbur, Robert E. (Bert) Swain (who is credited with the original concept in 1925), and Eliot Mears met to discuss their ideas. Despite support from university officials and alumni, the idea was sidetracked by the Depression and World War II. Stanford Research Institute was finally launched in 1946, coincidentally the year of Eliot Mears's death.

Gladys Mears had a deep interest in music and performed locally and for her family. She also taught music at Peninsula School in Menlo Park.

The Mearses had three daughters. The eldest, Helen, was 11 years old when the family moved into the house, and her sister Dorothy was 7. Three years later, Julianne was born. The older sisters recall climbing the Stanford foothills to picnic under the oak trees, and exploring the house's attic, finding a secret passage that led under the eaves of the house.

Helen Mears graduated from Palo Alto High School and attended Oberlin College in Ohio for two years. She transferred to Stanford, graduating in 1937 in graphic arts. Dorothy graduated from Stanford in 1941 in psychology, having studied with Lewis Terman. Julianne received an A.B. in music in 1951.

In 1941, Helen Mears married Weldon B. Gibson, a student of her father's who graduated in 1938 from Washington State and received an M.B.A. in 1940 and a Ph.D. in 1950 from Stanford. Gibson was one of the founders of Stanford Research Institute, a nonprofit subsidiary of Stanford incorporated in 1946 to provide specialized research services to businesses, foundations, and government agencies. (In 1970, Stanford's Board of Trustees voted to separate SRI from Stanford.)

By 1947, Gibson was chairman of SRI's international programs and later was president of SRI International. Starting in the 1950s, he helped make SRI a world leader in applied research. By the 1970s, he had set up an SRI-Moscow conference and led a large-scale mission to China. In many ways, his international affiliations continued the traditions fostered by his father-in-law, of building important associations between the Stanford community and the world beyond.

After the Gibsons moved into the house, in 1960, Gladys Mears lived with them until her death, in 1979. Memorable events held at the house include Dorothy's

Multipaned windows in the dining room were typical of Charles Sumner's designs. The arched cabinets on each side hold glassware and china.

wedding to Oliver Allen in 1942, numerous receptions and social gatherings for Stanford Research Institute staff and international visitors, and annual family Thanksgiving feasts.

Many of the grandchildren of Eliot and Gladys Mears are commemorated at the house by concrete stepping-stones that lead from the back door to the garden, each engraved with a grandchild's name and date of birth.

Hoot Gibson died in 2001. Helen Gibson continues to live in the house. ❋

Helen Gibson stands under stone arch surrounding the front door. Stones came from rubble from the 1906 earthquake.

Brass ceiling fixture in dining room and wall sconce are original.

Wood-paneled study with fireplace was used by both Eliot Mears and his son-in-law Hoot Gibson. Gibson's portrait hangs over the fireplace.

Paneled front door has Gothic arch and a small window with a wrought-iron insert.

SOURCES

Gibson, David. Interview with Marian Adams (7 February 2005).

Gibson, Helen Mears. Conversation with author (12 November 2004).

Gibson, Helen Mears, and Dorothy Mears Allen. Conversations with author (30 October 2002).

Gibson, Weldon B. "In Loving Memory of Gladys Chute Mears." Prepared with her daughters Helen M. Gibson, Dorothy M. Allen, and Julianne M. Marx (1980–81).

Gibson, Weldon B. *SRI: The Founding Years: A Big Step at the Golden Time.* Los Altos, California: Publishing Services Center (1980).

Mears, E. G. "California's Attitude toward the Oriental," *Annals of the American Academy of Political and Social Science* (November 1925): 199–213.

Mears, E. G. "The Institute of Pacific Relations," *Stanford Illustrated Review* 20, no. 1 (October 1927): 18–19.

Memorial resolution: Eliot Grinnell Mears (1889–1946). Stanford University Academic Council.

Mogens Mogensen [architectural firm]. Blueprints for renovations (1960). Stanford University Maps and Records.

Sumner, Charles K. Blueprints for house and instructions for workers building the house (1926); blueprints for alterations (1935). Stanford University Maps and Records.

Turner, Paul V., Wattis Professor of Art at Stanford. Tour of house's exterior with author (spring 2003).

"Weldon B. Gibson" [obit]. *Campus Report* (9 May 2001): 2.

PHOTOS

Mears, Gibson collection; Helen Gibson at door, Therese Baker-Degler; 1920s photo of three houses, Griffing family collection; all others Leni Hazlett.

Helen Gibson's watercolor of the house appeared on a 1967 Christmas card and in her husband's book on SRI.

In the mid-1920s, new houses at 593, 607, and 635 Gerona Road await landscaping and tree cover. View is from Santa Maria Avenue.

607 Gerona Road

BYRON FEIG

1926 ~ Spanish eclectic period style

ARCHITECT	OWNERS
Birge M. Clark	Miles—Adams—Spaeth

BY DICK BENNETT, ANN KAY,
AND VIRGINIA MANN

In 1926, while still in his early 30s, Palo Alto architect Birge M. Clark designed this Spanish-style house whose red tile roof, cream-colored stucco walls, and picturesque details would become his architectural signature over a long career.

Clark's artistry starts at the inset front door, with its molded stucco overhang, which suggests a shell design. On the left side of the front door is a lantern light of twisted wrought iron. Echoing the light's style, a masonry grille covers a small upstairs window in a bedroom closet, and a similar but larger grille provides privacy to a ground-floor bathroom. Above the front door, a wrought-iron grille covers a large window. Glazed tile squares in a subdued green openwork design vent the attic and the under-roof spaces. To the left of the front door, an unobtrusive stucco staircase serves as a private entrance to the upstairs bedrooms.

Inside the house, the ground floor comprises living and dining rooms to the right of the entry, as well as the kitchen, a bedroom, two bathrooms, and a study. A handsome staircase leads up from the entry hall to six bedrooms (one a former porch), two bathrooms, and a sewing room. In the dining room, the house's original dark-stained ceiling beams and woodwork have been preserved. In the large living room, the wrought-iron chandeliers enhance the Spanish-style motif, though the iron curtain rods were replaced long ago.

In the back garden, a U-shaped bench includes several pieces of mosaic that are, presumably, Memorial Church rubble from the 1906 earthquake. Plantings include a circle of mature redwoods and a large, beautiful sycamore that shades a deck added in 1963. In front of the house, olive trees edge the circular driveway, and a large Monterey pine spreads over the center of the drive.

The Owners

~Walter Richard Miles~

In 1926, Miles commissioned Birge Clark to design the house, which cost about $16,500. At the time, Miles, a professor of experimental psychology and a widower with three children, was renting a house at 739 Santa Ynez from Mrs. Herbert Hoover.

Miles, who was born in Silverleaf, North Dakota, in 1885, earned bachelor's degrees at Pacific College in Oregon in 1906 and Earlham College in Indiana in 1908, then a master's and a doctorate at the University of Iowa in 1910 and 1913, respectively. From 1914 to 1927, he was a psychologist at the Carnegie Institution's Nutrition Laboratory in Boston. He joined the Stanford faculty as

At the front entrance, Spanish details include paneled door in sculptural archway, grille over upstairs window, and wrought-iron light.

professor of experimental psychology in 1922. His first wife, Elizabeth Kirk, whom he had married in 1908, died in 1925.

In 1927, Miles married Catharine M. Cox, a research associate in the Psychology Department, who had earned three degrees from Stanford: bachelor's (1912), master's (1913), and doctorate (1925). They had two children. Catharine (1890–1984), who had an active and varied career, taught German at College of the Pacific in San Jose and at Stanford from 1914 to 1923. In 1919 and 1920, she was in charge of child feeding in Berlin for the American Friends Service Committee. In the 1920s and '30s, she collaborated with Lewis Terman on longitudinal studies of the gifted and on studies of gender differences in personality.

While at Stanford, Walter Miles worked with Lewis Terman, Calvin Stone, and E. K. Strong on the Stanford Late Maturity Study, the first systematic large-scale study of age and its relation to human performance. Their findings—that chronologically mature people do not demonstrate impaired performance until age 60—revolutionized the idea that old age began at 40.

Professor Miles was keenly interested in the work of photographer Eadweard Muybridge, whom Leland Stanford had hired in 1872 to provide photographic evidence that a trotting horse—a "horse in motion"—has all four feet off the ground at one point in its stride. In July 1878, Muybridge published his first series of photographs, taken by multiple cameras at split-second speeds, proving Stanford's theory. In 1928, Professor Miles hosted a 50th anniversary event at the Stanford Museum to commemorate Muybridge's work.

In 1931, Yale granted Miles an honorary degree, and he joined the Yale faculty the same year. Catharine Cox Miles, who had not progressed beyond the title of research associate at Stanford (perhaps because of Stanford's strict nepotism policies at the time), was appointed clinical professor of psychology at Yale.

During his long career, Walter Miles published some 70 works on the effects of nutrition, alcohol, and age on the human condition and ability. (Folklore or perhaps fact states that Professor Miles conducted experiments with rats in an outdoor maze, observing their behavior by peering down from the upstairs porch.) During World War II, Miles

From the front entrance, long staircase leads upstairs to bedrooms, baths, and a sewing room.

Psychologist Walter Miles had wide-ranging interests; in a portrait, he's shown with his invention of goggles for pilots flying at night.

introduced the use of red goggles that shortened the time necessary for pilots to acquire night vision. After retiring from Yale in 1953, he taught at the University of Istanbul, and in the late 1950s became scientific director of the Navy's Submarine Medical Research Laboratory at New London, Connecticut, retiring at 80. He died in 1978.

With Lewis M. Terman, Catharine Miles coauthored a 1926 Stanford Press book, *The Early Mental Traits of Three Hundred Geniuses.* They also wrote *Sex and Personality: Studies in Masculinity and Femininity,* published by McGraw-Hill in 1936.

After joining Yale's faculty, Walter and Catharine Miles became absentee landlords, renting 607 Gerona Road to students and to U.S. servicemen during World War II. The house was sold to Harlen Adams in early 1946.

~Harlen Martin Adams~

Adams, who was born in 1904 in Provo, Utah, had a peripatetic career, earning his Ed.D. from Stanford in 1938 while also serving as chairman of the English Department and director of speech arts at Menlo Junior College from 1935 until 1939. Beginning in 1936, he was also acting instructor of education at Stanford. After teaching for several years at Chico State College, he returned to Stanford in 1943 as assistant professor of speech and education. In 1946 he returned to Chico, where he served as dean of the schools of arts and sciences and of education, and as executive dean of the college. Eight months after he and his wife, Lois Carman Adams, bought the house—apparently without ever living in it—they sold it to Carl and Sheila Spaeth for $17,500. Adams died in 1997.

~Carl Bernhardt Spaeth~

Spaeth was born on May 3, 1907, in Cleveland, Ohio. He attended Dartmouth College, from which he graduated in 1929. As a Rhodes scholar, he attended Exeter College of Oxford University, earning a bachelor of arts degree in 1931 and a bachelor of civil law in 1932. From 1933 to 1940, he taught at Temple, Northwestern, and Yale universities.

Between 1940 and 1946, Carl Spaeth filled a series of U.S. State Department assignments in Venezuela, Uruguay, and Washington. He was special assistant to the assistant secretary of state for American republics affairs when, in 1946, he accepted President Donald Tresidder's offer to become dean of the Stanford Law School.

As the new dean, Spaeth made significant changes in both faculty and curriculum. The majority of the professors he recruited were not much older than their students. (Many of the pre-Spaeth faculty, including Professor Stanley Morrison, who served as law secretary to Justice Oliver Wendell Holmes, dated back to the early days of the university.) Spaeth also enlarged the law curriculum, inaugurated a student-run law review, and brought eminent professors from East Coast schools to teach in the summer. He died in 1991.

Carl Spaeth

English by birth, Sheila Spaeth had grown up in London, spending summers in Scotland. When she saw the house her husband had purchased, she was

Earthquake fragments from first Stanford church form a U-shaped low bench for plants or sitting; close-up shows detail.

confronted by an unfamiliar style—red Spanish tiles and thick stucco walls—and the challenge of decorating a Spanish-style house with English antiques. "We had to have somewhere to live," Carl Spaeth said, explaining why he had bought it.

When the Spaeths arrived, after a cross-country drive with their children in a 1939 Pontiac, the house was not ready for occupancy. Only recently had it been vacated by an unknown number of student residents. Professor Miles's rat maze was gone, but evidence of the previous 15 years remained. Students had occupied the upstairs bedrooms and the garage (where one bed had been tucked into a storage cabinet); another student had lived in the small sewing room, sleeping atop the table designed for cutting fabric.

Undaunted, Sheila Spaeth, who before her marriage, in 1931, had worked in the world of London theater production and costume design, looked upon the house as a set to strike for a play when its run was over. She enlisted the talents of her longtime friend Alice Eurich, wife of the university's vice president, Alvin C. Eurich.

Following Sheila Spaeth's design, Alice Eurich first removed the dark bookcases that flanked the living room fireplace, then removed the dark ceiling beams and painted the ceiling and walls white. She also replaced the heavy iron curtain rods with lighter hardware.

The door that led directly to the kitchen from the front hall was walled in to better define the entry to the living room on the right and to the study and staircase on the left. Throughout the house, the hardwood floors were cleaned and refinished. Sheila Spaeth made new drapes and curtains on a hand-operated sewing machine.

When the Spaeths bought the house, it had a cactus garden, which they decided to dismantle. Mrs. Spaeth commissioned eminent landscape architect Thomas Church to design the grounds, but his estimate to carry out her plan was more than the cost of the house, so it was never planted. At some point, she built a fence around the property.

The Spaeths frequently entertained local and visiting faculty at their home. For summer luncheons and faculty poker games, they constructed a large round redwood table within the redwood grove. Just outside the living and dining rooms, they added a large deck to the back garden to continue their tradition of hospitality and entertainment, including Sheila Spaeth's superb suppers of poached salmon in white wine sauce. Carl Spaeth enjoyed dancing; their son, Grant, played the piano for singing and dancing; and their daughter, Laurie, did a mean Charleston. Laurie fondly remembers her birthday parties at the house, especially the year her mother rented the movie *It Happened One Night,* during a time when showing a movie at home was unusual.

In 1963, the Spaeths extended the dining room to make space for a grand piano; it sat in a bay window made by enlarging a small window looking onto the garden. In the living room, another small window was enlarged to bring in more light at the front of the house.

Although the house did not suffer serious damage in the 1989 Loma Prieta earthquake, the dining room extension required structural reinforcement.

Birge Clark's design made a generous allowance for storage. One of Sheila Spaeth's favorite closets has a long rod for draping tablecloths, with enough space below for wine storage. And the kitchen contained what she recognized as an English larder (known in California as a cooler). The larder no longer exists, and the kitchen has been updated with larger ovens. The Spaeth hospitality remains. Sheila Spaeth, 99 years old in February 2005, still enjoys living in her house with her daughter. ❋

Decorative openwork tile in roof peak has utilitarian purpose: venting the attic.

SOURCES

Bartholomew, Karen, Claude Brinegar, and Roxanne Nilan. *A Chronology of Stanford University and its Founders* [Muybridge]. Stanford Historical Society (2001).

Blueprints of house. Stanford University Maps and Records.

"Catharine Cox Miles." *Who's Who of American Women,* 4th ed. (1966–67).

"Harlen Adams." *Contemporary Authors Online.* The Gale Group (2000).

"Harlen Adams" [obit]. *Chico Enterprise-Record* (20 December 1997): A1, A12.

Memorial Resolution: Carl Bernhardt Spaeth (1907–91). Stanford University Academic Council.

Spaeth, Laurie. Conversation with Margaret McKinnon (February 2004).

Spaeth, Sheila and Laurie. Interviews with Virginia Mann (late 1990s); Bennett and Kay (spring 2003).

"Walter Miles" [obit]. *Washington Post.* (19 May 1978): B6 metro edition.

Who Was Who [Walter Richard Miles] 7 (1977–81), 8 (1982–85).

PHOTOS

Miles, Stanford Archives; Spaeth, *Stanford Quad*; all others, Leni Hazlett.

635 Gerona Road

BYRON FEIG

1926 ~ French country

ARCHITECT	OWNERS
John K. Branner	Guérard—Guerard—Goldstein

BY THERESE L. BAKER-DEGLER

"Being in this house...is a constant joy." —*Albert J. Guerard*

During more than 75 years, this early faculty house was inhabited by three generations of one family. The country-style *maison*, built in 1926–27, is unusual in that it strongly represents the architectural, cultural, and aesthetic tastes of Albert Léon Guérard, who was born in Paris in 1880 and came to the United States in 1906, and of his wife, Wilhelmina McCartney, whom he married in 1907.

For 35 years, Guérard (A. L. or Papa to his children and grandchildren) and his wife (Mina as A. L. called her, Mamina to everyone else) lived in the house, for some of the time with their daughter, Catherine (Therina), and son, Albert (A. J.). From 1961 until their deaths, in 2000 and 2002, respectively, Albert J. and his wife, Maclin Bocock, lived there. Their daughters, Collot, Nini, and Lundie, grew up in the house, and in turn their children—A. L. and Mamina's great-grandchildren—spent many summers and vacations at the house.

The older Guérards first came to Stanford in 1907, and A. L. served as an assistant and then associate professor of French. In 1913, they left for 11 years at Rice Institute in Houston and a year at UCLA. When the family returned permanently to Stanford in 1925, the children were aged 15 and nearly 11.

Documentation in the family's possession and in the Stanford Archives includes the plans, design, and descriptions of the building process and furnishing of the house in 1926 and 1927. Among these sources are A. L.'s diary for the years when the house was being built and first occupied; Mamina's essay ("A Defence for a French Salon") on how she furnished the salon in 1928–29, written three years after its completion; and Albert J.'s reminiscence in the 1990s of how the house was created. These sources clearly indicate the central roles of A. L. and Mamina in the development of their Stanford home.

Interest in design of the built landscape was not just a pastime for A. L. His son recalled: "I often found my father at his labor of love...pouring [sic] over maps of Paris and pondering changes that should be made in the city's streets and facilities." These interests led to French publications on urban design (such as *L'Avenir de Paris*, 1929). On the Guérards' return to Stanford in 1925, they chose to locate their house on Gerona Road, at the southern edge of the main campus, with a fine view of the hills.

From the beginning, A. L. and his wife held foremost in their minds an ideal image of an unpretentious, though bourgeois, house characteristic of those in the French countryside. The Guérards first engaged the architect Charles K. Sumner in early 1926 to develop the architectural plan, but his design of a "small castle with turrets" with an "elaborate gate" did not realize their ideal. By April, they had engaged John Kennedy Branner to design the understated and graceful house that we see today; plans were completed in May.

The house, built on about an acre of land, had 3,770 square feet of living space on two floors and cost $26,000. From the outside, its French character is unmistakable: French doors with full-length shutters on the first floor, decorative iron French balconies on the second-floor windows, the hip roof with three dormers in the front and one in the back. Also suggestive are the quoins on the outside corners of the house (most often made of stone but here duplicated in stucco), the balustrade on the top of the garage, the raised terrace in front of the house with its typically French metal table and chairs, and the gardens.

Inside the house, the French style continued in the ceiling moldings, the herringbone marquetry floors on the first floor, the living and dining room French doors, and the mirror and cast-concrete mantel above the fireplace. One unusual feature was a telephone room off the foyer that was built under the winding staircase. The staircase with its decorative iron banister led to four bedrooms on the second floor. The master suite comprised a bedroom, two decks, two dressing rooms, a bath, and a study with a Murphy bed. The third-floor attic with its cathedral ceiling and dormer

From the front of the house, unobstructed early view takes in hills to the west (now across Junipero Serra Boulevard).

Recently finished country-style French maison, built in 1926, stands alone on its Gerona Road lot.

windows was ideal for play as well as for storage.

While the house was under construction, the Guérard family spent the summer in Los Angeles. On their return in October, A. L.'s diary reports the progress on the house:

> *October 26, 1926:* Mina very happy about house.
> *Memoranda for November 1926:* House progresses slowly, but takes shape excellently.
> *December 9, 1926:* Perfect house.

By December 18 and 19, they were leaving their temporary quarters on Alvarado Row and moving to Gerona Road.

By the following summer, the Guérards had turned their new house into their home. They called it "Île de France." Again A. L.'s diary highlights this process:

> *January 27, 1927:* Penultimate inspection of house. Delighted.
> *January 29, 1927:* Unpack our Houston furniture. (A. J. busy in the attic with his trains.)
> *January 31, 1927:* On with arranging books. Dining room furniture arrives OK. Beautiful.
> *February 1, 1927:* Finish arranging library.
> *February 7, 1927:* Lamps arrive. House beautiful at night.
> *February 15, 1927:* Worst rain and windstorm I remember here. Mopping up house. Trees almost uprooted. Awake 2–3 a.m.
> *March 7, 1927:* 20 bills...from Branner. Going over extras. Tedious work.
> *May 4, 1927:* Garden taking shape. Pleasant consultation with Branner.
> *July 4, 1927:* Play tennis with children...and others. Tennis, croquet, and tea.

Early photographs of the house, with its symmetrical design and elegant simplicity, reveal how little it has changed over three-quarters of a century. Stanford architectural historian Paul Turner has noted that while the classic symmetry and simplicity are certainly characteristic of a French country house, these qualities also appear in the architecture of early American Georgian houses.

CREATING A FRENCH SALON

In a delightful essay, Mamina, a published author, retells her adventures in finding the proper furnishings for the salon. Initially, she believed that she could create it with items purchased in San Francisco and Los Angeles, but antiques were hard to find and beyond her means. She wanted as well to avoid the "cheap commercialized Louis Seize of certain hotel rooms...or in some wealthy American homes, the fragile gilt ball room chair of the Second Empire." These she described as artificial, gaudy, and banal. Instead, she sought "the sturdiness...of the most graceful products of the Eighteenth Century."

In 1928, her quest took her to Paris, where she first shopped the best-known areas for French antiques: the Faubourg St.-Honoré and the Faubourg St.-Germain. But what she saw as beautiful was beyond her budget. She reversed her course and looked at more modest furniture establishments but found that "the fresh gilt and vivid upholstery gave me the creeps."

By chance, on a walk down the Champs-Elysées, she entered a gallery to look at some paintings and realized that the rooms she was walking through were also furniture showrooms of an old and established firm, Mercier Frères. The chief decorator of the firm, M. Tendille, helped her select furnishings for her salon. When the first plan exceeded her budget,

> ...he led me through what seemed hundreds of rooms, up and down myriads of stairs. He picked out here and there the models that had been selected for my room. Occasionally, he offered a substitution: "This will give you the same effect and be much less expensive"...He was quite consoling when a dark chair took the place of a gilded one: "You don't want too much gold in your salon." I wondered what he would have said if I had been a millionaire?

Mamina Guérard and the family dog, Coco, on the day bed, which was among the furnishings she had bought in Paris.

The final array of furnishings included a *lit de repos* (day bed) upholstered in rose satin damask strewn with silver and blue flowers, with two companion chairs and a kidney-shaped table in front, a *guéridon* (low table) to go in front of the fireplace, a *grande bergère* (large wing chair) with a matching *pouf* (which could be combined to form a *chaise longue*), a Louis Quinze *canapé* (loveseat) of gilt wood with silk upholstery in beige with scrolls of rose and blue, petit point tapestry chairs in cerise with baskets of flowers, a card table with a blue damask top and four chairs with blue seats, rose taffeta curtains, low bookcases, and wall sconces.

Moreover, M. Tendille introduced her to a painter, M. Wirth, who showed her designs he would paint to fit the 8-foot-square wall panel facing the mirror and for a rug to be woven to her specifications. The painting would be a landscape similar to those of the 18th-century French painter and landscape artist Hubert Robert, with the "inevitable ruin, a scarcely less inevitable waterfall, the ubiquitous see-saw, lovelorn youths, dainty maidens, and ironical ducks." In the wall painting, the square structure on the left with the balustrade copies the one above the Guérard garage, which Mamina had the artist include in his bucolic scene. The Savonnerie rug, chosen from a drawing and woven to her specified size, has a Louis XVI design with a center medallion surrounded by roses. The price, she was told, would vary with the rug's size and thickness.

A detailed price list of all the furnishings, including rose taffeta curtains, vases, and two bookcases as well as the wall painting and the rug (the most expensive item) cost approximately $5,800 at the time (about $58,000 in today's dollars).

Mamina concludes her essay with reactions to the very attentive assistance she received from the French:

> It was a joy to work with men who strove in every way to help me realize my dream, and who could scarcely have given me more time or shown more courteous attention if I had spent several hundred thousand dollars. I like to think that they too feel pride and pleasure in the thought of the salon in a distant land, not unworthy of the great century from which it drew its inspiration.

She also describes the joyful arrival of the furnishings at 635 Gerona Road:

> Gradually the room took form as each chair or table reached its appointed place... In three hours, a miracle had taken place. The former non-descript "living room" had been transformed into an XVIIIth century "salon." Something we had dreamed about for years had become a reality.

In the living room, wall painting evokes 18th-century French landscape.

Other Parisian furnishings in the salon included card table topped with blue damask, and four matching chairs. Curtains are rose taffeta.

When Albert J. and his wife, Maclin, lived in the house, they added other French details, including a bust of Voltaire on the foyer table, which was often decorated for special events.

THE GUÉRARDS' SOCIAL WORLD

Five years after the "salon" had been furnished, Mamina reported that it was being used as she had hoped it would be—to support the social interaction of the family with their friends:

> The skepticism of some of our friends as to the "live-ability" of a period room has entirely vanished. I have been surprised at the evident pleasure with which huge football fellows have sunk into the soft silk cushions of the *lit de repos*. Uncouth high school boys stretch their arms, unafraid, over the curved back of the gilded *canapé*. Young girls do not hesitate to sit in front of the fire on the soft rug—a rug on which no one has ever dreamed of flicking ashes. There are forms of beauty that inspire respect without constraint or awe. I have yet to see a rough gesture or hear an ungracious word in that room.... If we selected a French XVIIIth century salon it was not because it was exotic, and not because it was historical: but simply because it was beautiful. We found in it the expression of a social life which has never been surpassed for cheerful refinement.

The grandchildren of A. L. and Mamina—A. J. and Maclin's daughters and of one of Therina's sons, Greg Pearson—have recalled their childhood visits to their grandparents. Papa was very clever with his hands. He created elaborate figures out of cardboard and other basic materials to delight his visiting grandchildren. These included a large ocean liner and a male figure named Uncle Waldo, with a handlebar mustache and a top hat. The grandchildren would play in the attic, and, when Therina's sons were also visiting, they would sleep there, too.

Greg Pearson and his cousin Collot recall their grandfather as a "scholar and gentleman." He would become very discouraged if the grandchildren had scuffed shoes, and he would insist on polishing them. When one of his eminent friends, Julian Huxley, visited the house, A. L. commented after he left that Huxley's pants had been crumpled while his had a lovely crease. Their grandmother supervised the house, screening telephone calls for A. L. and holding high expectations for the upkeep of the house. One anecdote that survives is that when David Packard, co-founder of Hewlett Packard, rented the Guérards' attic during his undergraduate days at Stanford, choosing to do housework rather than pay rent, Mamina would carefully supervise his polishing of the hardwood floors, pointing out parts of the floor that he had missed.

In the evening, A. L. would read to Mamina from 19th-century French novels as well as from the works of American writers such as Zane Gray and James M. Cain.

One of the very social features of the Guérard home was the tennis court at the back of the house, which A. J. and his sister, Therina, had insisted upon. A. J. explained that his parents regularly played tennis before breakfast, and he and his sister organized tournaments with their friends. A. J. also recalled track meets on Gerona Road and boxing matches in the attic. The front yard was used for croquet. He notes that girls would join the boys in play and often beat them. Those who were particularly fleet of foot included Helen Mears (Mrs. Gibson, who still lives at 593 Gerona Road), Ada Martin, and Shelley Smith.

A. J. Guerard was a great sports fan and followed the Stanford teams closely. "When Ernie Nevers and other football stars turned to basketball, then to track, so did we." Even

French still life in the entry hall includes a bust of Voltaire and a rooster.

Flanked by Lombardy poplars and with topiary shrubs out front, the house would look at home in France. (Poplars didn't survive.)

in later years, A. J. still remained an avid fan. "Until the very end, Saturday afternoon was sacred—he would be watching Stanford football on television," reported his former student and later Stanford colleague, Thomas Moser.

Collot and Lundie Guerard remember the front terrace and the salon as the family's favorite gathering places. Many special events took place chez Guerard. Collot, A. J. and Maclin's oldest daughter, organized a formal dance in 1962. She, Nini, and Lundie were all married in the rose garden.

STUDENT RENTERS

Shortly after the house was built, a room with bath was added behind the garage and rented to students. However, the most illustrious tenant, David Packard, rented the attic during his senior year at Stanford when he was the president of ASSU (Associated Students of Stanford University). He came to know A. L. and Mamina well. A. J. reported that when his mother was dying, David Packard came to visit her and told her that he was going to endow a chair in her deceased husband's name. (A. J. would later be appointed the Albert L. Guérard Professor of Literature).

The Owners

~Albert Léon Guérard~

The Stanford careers of Albert Léon and Albert Joseph, both literary scholars, nearly spanned the 20th century. Each lived in the Gerona Road house while on the faculty, and each made major contributions to the development of the humanities at the university.

A. L., born in 1880 in Paris, was educated at the University of Paris and the University of London; he became an *agrégé* at the Sorbonne in 1906. From 1907 to 1913, he served as assistant and then associate professor of French at Stanford. He returned to Stanford in 1925 after 11 years at Rice and a year at UCLA, and remained as a professor of both French and English until his retirement, in 1946.

His academic and intellectual interests ranged widely. Most of his 28 books were on historical topics, but others focused on literary themes, city planning, and political ideals (especially his support for an international language and world government). In his self-portrayal in *Twentieth Century Authors* (1942), A. L. writes that he put most of himself into his first book: *French Prophets of Yesterday: A Study of Religious Thought Under The Second Empire* (1913) and a few others with philosophical themes, but that he thought that his most useful books would be *The Life and Death of an Ideal: France in the Classical Age* (1928), *A Short History of the International Language Movement* (1922), and *A Preface to World Literature* (c. 1940). He also wrote extensively for magazines and journals.

In an article in *The Nation* (April 1946), he challenged Reinhold Niebuhr's contention that there was no real world community, stating that "There is a humanity common to all men; to defend it is our 'common cause.'" At the time of his retirement, he was working with other noted scholars on a "world constitution." He also completed a short history of France, defending the 2,000-year history of his homeland after its defeat in the Second World War. While his adult life saw Europe go through two devastating wars, he remained

Albert Léon Guérard in 1907, the year he arrived at Stanford and just before his marriage to Wilhelmina McCartney. At right, they walk on Governor's Lane. Eucalyptus trees are already a good size.

Garden was the setting for weddings of all three of the Guerard daughters.

idealistically optimistic that human communities could learn to live in peace. After his retirement, he completed a four-volume intellectual autobiography.

Albert Leon Guérard died in 1959, his wife in 1963. She graduated from the University of Denver in 1897 and received an M.A. in history from Stanford in 1909 while A. L. was an assistant professor. She wrote short stories and articles, the first of which was published in the *Atlantic Monthly*. She also worked for years on a lengthy novel, "Catherine," (the manuscript was never published) about her own mother's prominent family in Glasgow and how they had tried to stop her from marrying the American minister John McCartney. After they married, they returned to America (Ohio), raising Mamina and four brothers, each of whom, following their father, became a prominent Presbyterian minister. Her son, A. J., noted that he had tried at several points to help his mother finish her novel.

~Albert Joseph Guerard~

Albert Joseph, born in Houston in 1914 while his father was teaching at Rice, was nearly 11 when his parents moved back to Stanford. He attended Menlo School, then Palo Alto High School. He was not an exemplary student (though he won a national short story prize during high school), and A. L. had to convince President Ray Lyman Wilbur that his son would do well at Stanford. This proved accurate, as he graduated from Stanford in 1934 "with great distinction" and a Phi Beta Kappa key, and then went on to Harvard for a master's degree, which he received in 1935. After a year teaching at Amherst College, he returned to Stanford, completing his Ph.D. in 1938. (Along the way, he dropped the *é* from his name.)

From 1938 until 1961, he was a member of the Department of English at Harvard. He married Maclin Bocock in 1941, then served as a technical sergeant in the Psychological Warfare Branch of the U.S. Army during the Second World War. At Harvard his reputation as a fine teacher of creative writing developed, and many future prominent authors attended his courses. As one former student at Harvard, David Levin, recalled: "He treated us all as adults, as fellow-writers, rather than as pupils."

In 1961, after much consideration, he returned to Stanford as a professor of English. Within a few years, he was awarded the chair that David Packard had endowed to honor his father.

At Stanford, he helped to get funding to bring professional writers to campus to teach as part of the Voice Project, a controversial freshman writing program. When he was interviewed in 1979 about the effectiveness of having writers teach creative writing, he contended "so long as the writer teacher doesn't think of it as a matter of techniques to be passed on, tricks of the trade, formulas for success... Every genuine writer has a voice of his own—an inward voice that stems from his temperament as well as from experience. The experienced teacher listens to that voice, helps bring it out."

His students, both at Harvard and Stanford, included many future prominent authors including Robert Bly, Harriet Doerr, Ron Hansen, John Hawkes, Alice Hoffman, Jonathan Kozol, Maxine Kumin, Alison Lurie, Frank O'Hara, and John Updike. Alice Hoffman described in a letter the impact of both Albert and Maclin on her: "Would I have been a writer had I not met you? The truth is, I'm not sure. Certainly, I would not have been the same writer."

In 1965, he started the first freshman seminar program, which continued for 13 years. Later he founded the interdisciplinary Ph.D. program in modern thought and literature. He was the winner of two distinguished teaching awards at Stanford.

Like his father, A. J. was "passionately interested in the world around him," stated Thomas Moser. A. J.'s writings included both novels and literary criticism. His nine novels have various themes: *Maquisard* and *Night Journey* relate to his World War II intelligence experiences, *Hotel in the Jungle* is a mixture of history and myth, *The Exiles* is a novel of political intrigue set in Latin America, and *The Bystander* is a psychological novel of love and self-deception set on the French Riviera. Six books of literary criticism explore the writings of a wide range of prominent authors including Joseph Conrad, Charles Dickens, Fyodor Dostoevsky,

Maclin and Albert Guerard, shown in 1939, when they were first engaged.

William Faulkner, André Gide, and Thomas Hardy. His memoir, *The Touch of Time: Myth, Memory, and the South*, includes a chapter "Stanford 1907–1979."

During her first year at Radcliffe, Maclin Bocock, raised in Virginia, heard A. J. lecture in her freshman English course and fell in love. Their 59-year marriage has been described by themselves, their daughters, and friends as a great love match. Maclin Bocock, a short-story writer, published in many literary quarterlies (including *The Southern Review* and *The Denver Quarterly*). Her first book, *Heaven Lies About*, a collection of short stories set in the South, was published in 1993, when she was 71. *A Citizen of the World,* a complete collection of her short stories, was published in 1999. At Stanford, she also taught a freshman seminar on writing. On their 50th wedding anniversary, in 1991, their daughters established the Maclin Bocock and Albert J. Guerard Creative Writing Prize in Fiction for Stanford undergraduates. Albert Guerard died in 2000 at the age of 86 in the same room where his father had died 41 years earlier. Maclin Bocock died in 2002 at the age of 81.

~Paul Goldstein~

In 2003, the house was sold to Goldstein, the Lillick Professor of Law, and his wife, Jan Newstrom Thompson, an art historian. They plan to maintain the French character of the house and its surroundings, though the tennis court will not survive.

Paul Goldstein received his A.B. from Brandeis in 1964 and his LL.B. from Columbia in 1967. His principal subjects are intellectual property law and international intellectual property law. Before coming to Stanford in 1975, he taught at the State University of New York at Buffalo. Jan Thompson, who holds a B.F.A. in graphic design and M.F.A. in printmaking from the University of Buffalo and received a Ph.D. in 1980 from Rutgers University, is a lecturer in art and design at San Jose State University. ❋

Sources

"Albert Guérard, Historian, Dead: Stanford Educator was 79. Led Battle of Words Against the 'Pharisees.'" *New York Times* (13 November 1959).

"Albert Guérard: When he becomes emeritus professor this summer he will lay aside only part of varied career." *Palo Alto Daily Times* (n.d., 1946).

"Albert Joseph Guerard, English professor, literary icon, dies" [news release]. Stanford News Service (15 November 2000).

Goldstein, Paul. Bio information from himself and http://stanford.edu (October 2004).

Guerard, Maclin Bocock [obit]. *Palo Alto Weekly* (15 January 2003): 11.

"Guérard, Albert Léon," in *Twentieth Century Authors,* ed. Stanley J. Kunitz and Howard Haycraft. New York: H. W. Wilson Company (1942): 583–584.

"Guerards' 50th anniversary marked by surprise gift." *The Stanford Centennial Campaign News* (Fall 1991): 1.

Guerard, Albert J. Video of memorial service (2 December 2000). Stanford Archives.

Guérard, Albert L. Diary (1926–27). Collection of Lundie Guerard.

Guerard, Collot, Lundie Guerard, and Greg Pearson. Discussions with the author (spring 2003).

Guerard, Collot, and Lundie Guerard. Correspondence and telephone calls with Margaret McKinnon (fall 2004).

Guerard, Maclin Bocock. Video of memorial service (January 2003). Stanford Archives.

Guérard, Wilhelmina McCartney, "A Defence for a French Salon." Unpublished manuscript (ca. 1932). Stanford Archives.

Guérard, Wilhelmina McCartney. "The Guerard Chronicles." Unpublished manuscript (n.d.). Stanford Archives.

Guérard, Wilhelmina McCartney. Price list of furniture (1928). Collection of Lundie Guerard.

Harvard University Press. *Autumn Announcements,* 1942: Short review of Albert L. Guérard: *The France of Tomorrow* (1942): 12; and a review by Albert Guerard Jr. (sic), Instructor in English, Harvard University, on Robert Bridges: *A Study of Traditionalism in Poetry* (1942): 21.

Hoffman, Alice. Letter to Albert and Maclin Guerard (23 May 1991). Collection of Lundie Guerard.

Memorial Resolution: Albert Léon Guérard (1880–1959). Stanford University Academic Council.

Thompson, Jan Newstrom. Bio details (October 2004).

Turner, Paul V., Wattis Professor of Art at Stanford. Tour of house with author (2003).

Photos

Guerard family.

792 Santa Maria Avenue

(FORMERLY LINDA VISTA AND FOOTHILL ROAD)

BYRON FEIG

1927 ~ Adobe style

ARCHITECT	OWNERS
Charles K. Sumner	Griffing—Beadle—Giese —Bennett

BY ANN KAY AND DICK BENNETT

When Charles K. Sumner designed this single-story adobe-style house for Elizabeth Perry Griffing in the summer of 1927, it must have seemed well out in the country, with few other houses in sight. The house was built on about four-fifths of an acre at the corner of Foothill Road and Linda Vista (now Junipero Serra Boulevard and Santa Maria Avenue). The building contract was $10,000, but final cost was about $16,000; the house was finished in March 1928.

The original watercolor that Sumner did for Elizabeth Griffing shows a low house set on a gentle rise with little vegetation around it. Early photographs taken looking east show the Ryan Lab, on Stanford Avenue near today's Raimundo Way. Photos over several years continued to show a dirt street in front of the house. Today a tangle of oaks and wild growth surrounds the property, shielding it from view.

The footprint was an H shape, with utility room, small kitchen, and a master bedroom with two closets and bath in one wing, and two bedrooms and a bath in the other. The master bedroom had doors to the dining room and the front porch; the bedroom in the opposite wing had a matching door to the porch.

The dining and living rooms made up the crossbar of the H, with front and back porches running the length of the crossbar. Across the front porch was an arbor framework that would eventually support a beautiful purple trumpet vine. The front door opened directly into the living room, which had a Dutch door out to the back porch.

An unusual feature specified in the blueprints was a Napanee baking cabinet built into the kitchen cabinetry. This cabinet was perhaps the most modern baking appliance of its day. It had a built-in flour sifter with special hinges to lift it out and over the pull-out enameled shelf that added to the counter space, as well as special bins and a wire shelf for cooling baked goods. A rolltop pulled down to hide any clutter, much like an appliance garage today. Ed Griffing remembers his mother regularly making bread at home.

Surrounded by uncultivated soil, house (about 1928) is not far from other new construction, including (far right) Mears house at 593 Gerona Road. Two years later, landscaping is already filling in (below), and another house has appeared on Gerona.

The kitchen itself was very small. It had a California cooler and a cupboard with sliding doors that rolled on ball bearings; it still worked smoothly when the present owners acquired the house. This cupboard was built from the Napanee cabinet's redwood shipping crate. When the kitchen was remodeled in 1995, the address for shipping and description of the cabinet were discovered stamped on the back side of the cupboard.

Other striking features of the house are the high ceilings: 14 feet in the living room and 9½ feet in the dining room. All the ceilings have hand-hewn and hand-adzed redwood beams. In the living room, a 25-foot beam stretches the length of the room with no tie rods. Ceilings in the bedrooms are lower, just 7½ feet to the bottom of the beams. The dining room, library, and bedrooms all have their original copper, brass, and iron light fixtures; the dining room ones still have their mica shades. Rounded fireplaces, originally brick but now plastered, nestle back-to-back in corners of the living and dining rooms. Every room has a small niche in the wall, harking back to earlier Spanish times when a religious statue would have been placed there.

Mica shade on dining room light fixture casts a warm glow.

Handmade Mexican tiles, 11 inches square and 2 inches thick, pave the living room floor. Slightly larger tiles were used for the front and back porches. In the rest of the house, floors are fir planks in 5-, 7-, and 9-inch widths. These planks run the length of each room without a joint. Redwood lintels, heavy redwood-plank doors, wrought-iron hardware made to the architect's designs, and 2-foot-thick walls with deep redwood window sills complete the adobe feeling. Elizabeth Griffing wrote that Sumner "went down to Santa Barbara researching items for [the house]."

The original blueprints specified two other rather unusual features: a bathroom and a concrete pit (still extant) in the two-car garage. Elizabeth Griffing later wrote, "And the garage was such fun, with the sunken service pit, to change oil, and the sunken Standard Oil gas tank." According to her son, Ed, the pit was for his father (Stanton Griffing) to work on the underside of a car. A gas pump inside the garage was used to fill up before going on trips. In her diary, Mrs. Griffing recalled one trip: "Stanton went over to the beach with his trailer and loaded it up with beach sand for Ed's sandbox which he had made back of the redwood logs used as a back stop for autos. It was right next to the vegetable garden." Both pump and tank were later removed, but the vegetable garden is still there.

Though Ed Griffing was only 7 when the family moved away, in 1941, he still remembers different vendors delivering milk, vegetables, and meat. Coal was delivered down a chute near the front right side of the house. Other memories were of an evergreen to the east of the driveway, a beautiful trumpet vine, and climbing in a pepper tree in front. The redwood tree the Griffings planted on the east

From the back of the house, view extends east as far as Ryan Lab, on Stanford Avenue.

side now takes four people to reach around it!

Mrs. Griffing was a keen gardener. Thirty years later, in the early 1970s, she recalled in her diary many of the plants in the yard including plumbago, abutilon, 'Beauty of Glazenwood' climbing rose, pampas grass, lemon verbena, avocado, asters, a fig tree, olives, redwoods, "and the grape arbor on the redwood rafters over the porch, and the big cactus plants at the corner of the front steps." She ended her list with, "A beautiful place. I wonder if the redwood and olives are still there and what it looks like now."

The Owners

~Elizabeth Perry Griffing~

Mrs. Griffing was born in 1891 and received her bachelor's degree from Simmons College in 1914 and her M.S. in physiology from Stanford in 1920. She later worked for 13 years as a research associate in the Food Research Institute. Her friends included David Starr Jordan and J. E. Wallace Sterling. How she came to build on the campus is not known. She did look back with such nostalgia and pride that a friend said you could sense the house was happy. She died in 1973 in Palm Springs; Stanton Griffing had died in 1963.

~George Beadle~

Beadle was born in Wahoo, Nebraska, in 1903. He graduated from the University of Nebraska, receiving a B.S. in agriculture in 1926 and an M.S. in 1927; his Ph.D. was from Cornell. In 1925, he married Marion Hill; their son, David, was born in 1931. Subsequently, Beadle was at California Institute of Technology, then Paris and Harvard. In 1937 he came to Stanford, where he remained until returning to Cal Tech in 1946; the Beadles lived in the house from 1941 to 1946. In 1961, he became president of the University of Chicago. Beadle died in 1989 in Pomona.

George Beadle, a geneticist, shared the 1958 Nobel Prize in physiology/medicine with Edward Tatum and Joshua Lederberg. Their work, which led to the unraveling of the structure of DNA, was done while all three were at Stanford (1937–46).

Ted Giese, son of a subsequent owner, described Beadle as having "acute intelligence, some humor and whimsy, no BS formality even though by then he was a renowned scientist." A colleague, Norman H. Horowitz,

George Beadle, during his time at Stanford.

When the house was built, fireplaces in living room (right) and dining room (far right) were exposed brick.

wrote a moving memoir of Beadle that described many aspects of his life at Stanford. "Beets," as he was called, grew up on a farm and "retained for the rest of his life the skills he learned as a gardener and beekeeper, and his handiness with tools."

Gardening was one of his great pleasures. During World War II, his victory garden covered the entire front yard and provided enough produce for more than two families. One year he decided to let the banana squash grow to see how big it would get. The biggest was 50 pounds, with two others over 25 pounds. Besides sweet corn, he grew popcorn, a great favorite, and carrots. His grad students worked in the garden. He also kept bees on the west side of the house. Beadle especially enjoyed working with his hands; his son, Dave, remembered that one of the first things his father did when they moved in was build a small barbecue off the back patio.

On Sundays the house was filled with friends over for barbecued steaks and roasted corn. After homemade fruit ice for dessert, the men would stretch out on the living room floor and nap while the women did the dishes. Sometimes they went up the hill, built a fire, and had fried egg sandwiches. Norman Horowitz wrote about a lab picnic one summer day at the beach. "To save gas, we bicycled, huffing and wheezing (we had no gears then). The only difference between Beets and the rest of us was that he was carrying a watermelon on his handlebars."

Dave, who was 10 when they moved in, remembered being excited about the house itself: "the hand forged hardware, all the redwoods and living on the edge of the hills." He was able to wander over the hills as far as Felt Lake.

During the war years, soldiers went by on Junipero Serra on foot, in trucks, or on motorcycles. One of his favorite places to play, when the soldiers weren't using it, was Camp Page Mill, a training camp. He swung on a rope over a creek, and he and his friends picked up brass shell casings. Above Moffett Field, a training camp for balloons and blimps, Dave counted 13 balloons and 3 blimps in the sky at once. Hershey bars were hard to get, but with the campus filled with Army cadets and Navy V12 men, Dave and his friends stood outside the PX in the basement of Encina Hall and got the men to buy Hershey bars for them. George Beadle was an air-raid warden, and Dave was mobilized to be a messenger and collect scrap iron.

For two years, Dave went to Stanford Elementary School, on the present site of the Pearce Mitchell condo-

After the house was renovated in the mid-1990s, fireplaces got a coating of plaster but are otherwise unchanged.

miniums. After Lou Henry Hoover's death, in 1944, Herbert Hoover donated their house to the university for use as the president's residence and rented one at 576 Gerona, whose backyard touched the Beadles'. Cutting across the Gerona lawn on the way to school, Dave "looked in the window and saw Herbert Hoover, with a cherubic round face, working at his typewriter."

Dave Beadle's memories included keeping goats on the Junipero Serra side of the house and chickens on the other side of the property. Hydrangeas grew from the house to the goat house, and a beautiful purple trumpet vine bloomed every May on the front arbor. Beadle loved corn and planted different kinds including a small Mexican variety that gave him the earliest sweet corn at Stanford. Apricots and plums from nearby orchards were sulfured and placed on large cookie sheets covered with cheesecloth, then dried on the woodshed roof. Sometimes they made apricot sun jam. The prunes were soaked in lye and canned. They also cured their olives. To keep all these provisions, they rented a cold-storage locker in Palo Alto.

The house was furnished with Navajo rugs, his mother upholstered an armchair in blue denim, and curtains were made from cotton chicken feed sacks with the curtain rings being plastic leg rings from the chickens. Against a dining room wall was a reed organ with a picture painted by his father's sister, Ruth, on it. On the far end of the living room was an Iverson upright piano. Mrs. Beadle played both the organ and the piano while Dave played the violin.

George Beadle made two lovely mahogany tables for the dining room, one at each end. In summer, Dave's electric train lived on the front porch, and on hot nights the family sometimes slept there on folding army cots.

Just after the war, Beadle moved to Cal Tech and needed to sell the house, but only to another Stanford faculty member, so he arranged an exchange of houses, plus $1,841.75, with Arthur Giese, who then lived at 750 Amherst Street in College Terrace. This exchange took place July 1, 1946. As Ted Giese recalled, housing was difficult to find in 1946, and Dr. Beadle had an immediate buyer for the Giese house—the parents of George Paddleford, who owned the Olds/Cadillac agency in Palo Alto.

~Arthur Giese~

Giese was born in Chicago in 1904, and at the University of Chicago majored in zoology and botany, graduating with distinction and departmental honors in 1927. Starting graduate study at Chicago, he transferred to UC Berkeley in 1927. After spending the summer of 1929 at Hopkins Marine Station in Monterey, he was appointed an acting instructor at Stanford, where he received his Ph.D. in zoology in 1933. He became a renowned authority on marine invertebrate biology, cell physiology, protozoology, and photobiology, and continued to work in the Department of Biological Sciences even after his retirement, in 1970.

In 1946 when the Gieses moved into the house, their son, Ted, was 14 years old. He still recalls the thrill of moving in, especially the smells: the dust on the gravel driveway and paths, the cut grass and fragrant flowers in the heat. Dr. Giese planted pineapple guavas all across the front. Some guavas still grow on the property, though none in front. His mother planted 'Star of Holland' red roses and made jelly from them.

Tiles along wall of front patio are for each of the California missions.

Redwood gate closes off side of patio closest to driveway.

In 1950 the Gieses installed a General Electric sink, which was a top-loading dishwasher-and-sink combination. Though rusty, it was still working in 1994. Roman Gankin, an old Russian friend of Arthur Giese's, made the andirons for the living room fireplace. They use the same mission bell design as the front door knocker.

Mrs. Giese painted portraits, often two of the same person: one for the subject and the other (not always flattering) painted as she saw the person, for herself. One of her portraits was of Dave Beadle.

Since the Gieses had only one car, they rented the other garage space to a lady who had a beautiful green Packard, and later to a young man with a "brand new 1949 Oldsmobile convertible, cream with fragrant brown leather upholstery and the first Kettering V-8 engine. It was always a thrill to hear him fire it up and go down the driveway," Ted remembers.

Arthur Giese's regular schedule was to weed the garden at 6 a.m., eat breakfast and walk to Stanford at 7 to 7:15, work in the garden again when he got home, have dinner, and go back to school until 10 or 10:30. He had many talents. In addition to playing the cello and the flute, he tended a vegetable garden and small orchard of fruit trees. Many still remain. Each of his graduating students received a cutting from a venerable jade plant that still grows on the property today. He continued to live in the house by himself after his wife's death until his death, in 1994. Between his work at Stanford and his garden, the house got little attention.

~Richard Bennett~

When Bennett bought the house in 1994, he had retired. A 1952 Stanford graduate, he spent six years in the Navy as a helicopter pilot, then returned to Stanford for 26 years in the Development Office (fundraising). His final years were spent guiding the Centennial Campaign (1987–92), first as director of campaign planning and finally as associate campaign director.

The house's architect, Charles Sumner, had specified in the original blueprints that the house be bolted to the foundation. As a result, the house suffered little earthquake damage over the years. Unfortunately dry rot, termites, and wood-eating beetles were not so kind.

No major changes had been made to the house until 1994 to 1996, when Bennett and his partner, Ann Kay, made extensive repairs and alterations. They added a bedroom, bath, laundry, a front hall and open courtyard, and new entrance. An expanded kitchen encompasses the old service porch, two closets, and a bathroom. The architect was Robert Wylie, who was familiar with Charles Sumner's work and was able to keep the original style as much as possible. W. L. Butler was the contractor.

In addition to the original living room, dining room, and smaller bedroom, the house now has a kitchen large

On the front of the house, tiled steps rise to partially enclosed patio and wood-framed French doors. New master bedroom wing is at left; main entry is at far right.

enough for the owners to enjoy cooking together, a library replacing the former master bedroom, an office, two bathrooms, a laundry, and a new master bedroom. A 40-foot-long front hall (or solar loggia, as the architect calls it) replaced the front porch.

The 2-foot-thick walls proved to be hollow, so bookshelves and closets could be inserted into them. All the old doors were reused. Uplights in the living room brighten the high space. The old front door, complete with knocker, is now the door to the master bedroom. Following the original blueprints, which called for the brick chimneys to be limed, the fireplaces have been plastered.

The old driveway has been resurfaced with pavers similar to those in the Quad. Replicas of the altar tiles of the California missions decorate the courtyard, and colorful Mexican tiles were used for the risers on the steps leading to the new entry.

The garden is an ongoing and probably never-ending project. And yes, Elizabeth Griffing's redwoods and olives are still there. The owners collect and cure the olives and give them to friends.

Dick Bennett and Ann Kay were married in a surprise wedding in the garden, where the grandchildren have a secret path that leads to a tree house they built. The house is often filled with friends and family. As Charles Sumner described the houses he designed, this one has "a feeling of permanence… reasonable, obvious strength and durability. The various parts of the house appear happy and at peace together." ❋

Dining room, though updated, still has original light fixtures and redwood beam above doorway. Alcoves on each side display glassware.

SOURCES

Beadle, David. Weekend interview with current owners (13–15 May 2003).

Beadle, George. *Stanford Alumni Review* (February 1946).

Beadle, George [obit]. "George W. Beadle, 85, Geneticist and Nobel Prize Winner, Is Dead." *The New York Times* (12 Jun 1989): D13.

"George W. Beadle Nobel Prizewinner." *Engineering and Science* [Cal Tech] (November 1958): 17.

"George Wells Beadle." University of Chicago [press release] (5 January 1961).

"How Stanford Nobelists founded molecular biology on a red mold" [press release]. Stanford News Service (8 October 1991).

"Arthur Charles Giese" [obit]. *Campus Report* (4 May 1994).

"Biology Emeritus Professor Arthur Giese Dead at 89" [obit]. *Stanford Observer* (January 1994).

Giese, Ted. E-mail conversations, visits with current owners (1995–2004).

Griffing, Ed. Telephone conversation and e-mails with authors; photographs and copies of Elizabeth Griffing's journal.

Griffing, Elizabeth. Excerpts from her journal (1971–73).

Horowitz, Norman H. "George Wells Beadle, 23 October 1903–June 6, 1989." *Genetics*, the Biographical Memoirs of the National Academy of Sciences and the 1995 American Philosophical Society Year Book (1995): 45–54.

Kinsell, Seybert. "Unforgettable Teachers: George Beadle." *Stanford* magazine (November–December 2003).

Santa Clara County tax records: 1926–28.

PHOTOS

Beadle, Stanford News Service; historic photos, Griffing family collection; all others, Leni Hazlett and Margaret McKinnon.

1040 Campus Drive

(COUNTY ROAD, 538 MAYFIELD, 538 CAMPUS DRIVE)

BYRON FEIG

BY DAVID AND NATALIE WEBER

In 1891, at 32 years of age, Douglas Houghton Campbell arrived in Menlo Park to be professor of botany among Stanford's pioneer faculty. A year later, 30-year-old Robert Edgar Allardice arrived as professor of mathematics. Both lived for a year in Lauro Hall, a boarding house for faculty. In 1893 they, with Professors E. H. Woodruff and A. P. Carman, built a house on land that Campbell had leased at 33 Alvarado and formed a small club there, popularly known as "The Bachelors."

1914 ~ Italian Renaissance eclectic style

ARCHITECT	OWNERS
Walter H. Ratcliff Jr.	Campbell/Allardice —Sangiorgi—Hastie

By the time the lease on the Alvarado house was 20 years old and up for renewal, the house was owned 50 percent by Campbell and 25 percent each by Allardice and Vernon Kellogg, professor of entomology. It was worth about $7,500. In August 1913, the three asked to sell their house to the university and lease it back for one year while they "expected to build another house" on campus.

The first documentary evidence that the new house was finished appeared in the 1914 Palo Alto area directory, listing both Allardice and Campbell as living at "County Road." In January 1928, the road was renamed Mayfield and, later, Campus Drive. In 1997, when the university renumbered Campus Drive, the house number changed from 538 to 1040.

Sometime in 1914, the professors settled in, supported by Moy Yuen, the Chinese cook or "overlord." Each gentleman so effectively preserved his individual habits and privacy that a story circulated that a complete set of the works of Robert Louis Stevenson had been sold to each!

Campbell was reported to have built the new house for himself and a friend or two. His nephew, a geologist, lived there while attending classes at Stanford. Other short-term residents may have included E. T. Fisher, the university's head bookkeeper, Professor and Mrs. David L. Webster, and Professor and Mrs. W. D. Briggs (who later built the adjacent house, now 1050 Campus Drive).

The original design for the house, with plans dated December 1913, was by Walter H. Ratcliff Jr., who in 1912 had designed a house for Vernon Kellogg at 622 Cabrillo. Ratcliff (1881-1973) went into practice in 1908, after working with Bernard Maybeck and John Galen Howard. His work ranged from Berkeley's first skyscraper to commercial buildings and private residences.

The Campbell-Allardice house had many elements of Italian Renaissance eclectic style, including decorative eave brackets, stucco exterior, plaster balconies, and a small loggia on the rear façade. According to the original plans, windows were to be leaded glass with square panes.

The original lease with description of the 2-acre plot has not been found, though the property shown in 1998

Geraniums spill over rough-stone retaining wall along pathway up to back of garden.

Loggia off dining room faces circular bed in tree-sheltered back garden. The curved arches and composite capitals show Italian influence.

remodeling plans has the boundary extending 459 feet along Campus Drive from Constanzo Street, with the back of the lot sweeping uphill along the pedestrian path that comes down from Cooksey Lane.

The house was sited about halfway up the plot depth and within 25 feet of the west property line, leaving considerable area behind, in front, and to the east of the house. From Campus Drive, the driveway curves around a circular planting area with an ancient oak tree; originally, a walkway ran past the oak to the kitchen entrance. Because of the lot's upslope from the street, the front entrance is up a stairway and along an unroofed veranda running across the width of the house.

Inside, to the left of the spacious entry hall, the original dining room featured a stone hearth within a wood surround and mantel, and plaster walls within slender wood panels. French doors on the back side opened to a loggia facing the back garden; four columns with composite capitals supported its arches.

A pantry separated the dining room and kitchen, which had a back entrance. Near this entrance were a bedroom and bath for Moy Yuen, commonly called Jo or Joe, as well as stairs to the basement. The living room, on the back of the house off the entry hall, featured a brick hearth, a copper hood within a wood frame and mantel, and wood-paneled walls.

Professors Campbell, Allardice, and Kellogg were each to have a "chamber"—Campbell's upstairs, and bedrooms and baths for the other two on the west end of the first floor. (However, as Kellogg had already built his own house, one of the first-floor chambers may have been intended as a study for Allardice or to rent to a tenant.)

On the second floor, Campbell's chamber with balcony and bath faced the street, while his living room with balcony faced the back of the lot. It featured a brick corner fireplace with copper hood and trapezoidal wooden overmantel, wood cornice, and picture molding. A linen closet was in the hallway.

In the original 2,873-square-foot house, the stairway to the upper floor had 6 steps, a landing, and then 10 more

From the sunny patio, loggia offers shaded seating and cool tiles where the family cat can stretch out.

Decorative details on capital of loggia columns defy classification.

steps; beside the upper flight were four leaded-glass windows, somewhat tall and narrow.

The house had a small paved basement with the hot-water heater, furnace, a long storeroom (now a workshop), and an uphill crawl space. Because Professor Campbell disliked automobiles and refused to acquire one, the house never had a garage. His horse boarded elsewhere.

The construction specifications add a few details. The roof was to be of Aberdeen Star cedar shingles or tile. Window sashes were to be of sugar pine. Leading in the staircase windows was to be 5/8 inch wide. Much of the first floor was to have white oak flooring with a six-line oak strip border. Exterior and interior woodwork was to be redwood. A wood cornice serving as picture molding was to go in the chambers, upper hall, dining room, and second-floor living room. Ceilings of the first-floor living room and lower hall were to be beamed. And the gas line was to include emergency gaslight outlets in the kitchen and dining room.

Douglas Campbell installed the garden with a botanist's enthusiasm. From the front walk, a trail led past the kitchen and along a rock ledge to a gate at or near the current path up to Cooksey Lane. Another path circled from this trail, roughly midway between the back of the house and the property line. Outside the dining room loggia, a brick courtyard had a slightly raised circular planter with center fountain figure and a trellised pergola behind. The house and garden became Campbell's home while teaching and his base for traveling abroad, as he did so often in pursuit of his research studies.

He planted deciduous trees and shrubs, visible from the house and from below, along a stream (no longer extant) and up the slope; they produced a show of color and interesting character during each season. Fruit trees included almond, apricot, fig, quince, olive, peach, pear, and plum; the quince and plum remain. About 250 kinds of plants and bulbs were brought from around the world.

A friend wrote that no scythe or hoe was ever used, and Dr. Campbell "nourished it only by the life-giving pipe line from the campus lake." Further, the cook "loved the soil and had been liberally encouraged to use it as his taste suggested. And many were the surprises resulting from profitable exchanges with other cooks of the garden estates!"

"In his very old age, when even walking had become a struggle, Dr. Campbell's friends would sometimes come upon him inching slowly along but enjoying still the cathedral lanes of his forest."

After Campbell's death, his faculty colleague Ira L. Wiggins wrote: "He was keenly interested in growing things considered exotic in that part of the state and tried scores of introductions—only a few of which prospered. He was very proud of the few that did live on his protected hillside. He was proud, too, of the coast redwood he had planted as a nursery seedling less than 3 feet high in 1914, and which had attained a height of 126 feet and shaded a third of his front yard by 1950."

The Owners

~Douglas Houghton Campbell and Robert Edgar Allardice~

The two colleagues lived in the house until their deaths: Allardice in 1928 and Campbell in 1952, the last link to the pioneer faculty of the university.

Campbell, son of a Michigan Supreme Court judge, was born in Detroit in 1859; he earned his B.S. and Ph.D. from the University of Michigan in 1882 and 1886, respectively. After further studies in Germany, he taught at Indiana University for three years before moving to Stanford in 1891 with the university's first president, David Starr Jordan.

From his arrival on the campus, he explored its reaches, often on horseback. His first book, *Mosses and Ferns* (1895), came largely from these explorations, and he became the leading American plant morphologist. He was also a talented artist, producing accurate, charming sketches in pen and ink and watercolor of objects and places about the world that especially interested him. He left a large collection of his watercolors to Stanford.

Douglas Houghton Campbell

Robert Edgar Allardice

His memorial resolution notes that he was known for his Old World courtliness: "for his great dignity of person coupled with a sincerity that won respect from students and colleagues alike." From his teens, a trim mustache, frequent boutonniere, and pince-nez glasses characterized his appearance. Widely traveled (the Caribbean, Europe, North Africa, Southeast Asia, and Hawaii), he also maintained a broad interest in art, music, and literature.

After his death, garden writer Albert Wilson wrote:

> His faithful partner on many an excursion was his spirited mount; together they scented out and carefully tracked down treasures that were hidden from everyone else. Occasionally they would come upon a certain little seasonal stream that stole from the southwest hills [San Juan Hill] into the campus. Along about 1910, let us say, one sunny springtime afternoon these two, cantering up the road, found along this stream a lush population of cattails, water cress, lupines, and dock. Their hearts were singing with contentment, and the frogs joined in. On the right was a gentle slope covered with barley which would soon lose its freshness and turn dry, yellow and hot. On the left the slope was steeper and cooler; at its base stood a little grove of deciduous oaks, and farther along a young evergreen oak. Between them and a little way up the slope was a magnificent specimen of the deciduous valley oak, *Quercus lobata*, with a "broad crown of tortuous branches and weeping sprays."

Professor of mathematics Robert Allardice, shown in a 1920s photo, relaxes on the loggia.

Near that oak, Campbell and Allardice built their house.

Allardice was born in Edinburgh, Scotland, in 1862 and graduated from the University of Edinburgh, where he was a brilliant instructor. When appointed to Stanford at age 30, he "had already earned the reputation of a mathematician of unusual distinction." He was important to the academic development of the university and in its social life. Campbell described Allardice as "a man of remarkable intellectual gifts and wide culture [who] was an admirable talker with a fund of interesting and amusing anecdotes, and he had a keen interest in games of various kinds...and had a large circle of devoted friends." He golfed, cycled, hiked in the mountains, visited Europe and the South Seas.

In 1899, he introduced golf to the campus when he formed the Machrihanish Golf Club and laid out a nine-hole course above the lake, Lagunita, between the Cooksey and Lathrop residences (now roughly the area of student residences along Campus Drive East near Junipero Serra Boulevard).

~Roberto Benaglia Sangiorgi~

A professor of Italian, Sangiorgi had lived on campus before moving into the house in the spring or summer of 1954. He was born in Italy in 1901 and reportedly bore the title of count. He earned his master's in 1935 and doctorate in 1944 from the University of California. After teaching in the Bay Area from 1927 to 1939, he came to Stanford as instructor in 1940 and served as professor of Italian from 1943 until he retired, in 1965. Music was his prime avocation, and he served at one time as director of the San Francisco Cantoria A Capella Choir.

He and his first wife had three children, comfortably filling the house. After Mrs. Sangiorgi died, in 1969, he frequently traveled back to Italy and Spain, and on one such trip he met Silvana Laurelli, who became his second wife. After 1965 he resided most of the time in Rome, renting rooms in his campus house to several students each year and making occasional visits but not living there again.

In 1995, the house (which the renters called "The Villa") was sold to Trevor and Lynda Hastie. Professor Sangiorgi and his wife returned for a last visit to the house, where they enjoyed dinner use with the Hasties. Professor Sangiorgi died in Rome in 1998, aged 97.

~TREVOR J. HASTIE~

Trevor and Lynda Hastie moved into the house in 1995 with their two children. They were both born in South Africa, and he received his M.S. in 1983 and Ph.D. in 1985 from Stanford. After working at AT&T Bell Labs for several years, he was appointed to the Stanford faculty in 1995 as associate professor of statistics and of health research and policy. The Hasties have made extensive alterations to the house.

ALTERATIONS AND RENOVATIONS

Sometime before about 1970, the shingle roof was replaced with red tiles. The Sangiorgis added a brick bread oven to the kitchen, with flue access on the back side of the dining room fireplace. The wall and door between the pantry and kitchen were removed. Removing the linen closet in the upper hall gave access to the attic area over the kitchen; it is now used as a guest bedroom.

In late January 1956, while the Sangiorgis were away, a fire broke out in the house. This calamity gutted most of the interior and destroyed all the furniture; only the kitchen and one upstairs room escaped destruction. A charred page was found as reminder of a book manuscript on which Professor Sangiorgi had been working.

After the fire, architect Morgan Stedman of Palo Alto designed a major renovation involving new windows, frames, doors, wiring, foundation vents, and furnace; enclosure of the loggia and removal of its doors to the dining room; replacement of the plaster balconies with wooden ones; adding steel beams above the living room to support the fireplace in the bedroom above; and relocation of the stairs to the second floor as a single flight up from the front door. On the west end, a flat roof replaced the pitched one. The former roof slope is still visible today beneath the whitewashed finish.

The 1989 Loma Prieta earthquake significantly damaged the kitchen, the two-sided fireplace, and the foundation wall on the east side. In July 1990, structural engineer Charles E. Philips and contractor Delmer Imhof prepared plans and a construction sheet covering, besides the structural work, new redwood decking and stairs to replace the walk on the front and left side of the house, strengthening of the two-sided fireplace and sealing off the kitchen bread oven, and new exterior stucco used in the renovation to match the existing stucco.

When the Hasties bought the house, they wanted to expand and modernize it while keeping its Italian style intact. In December 1997, plans by architect Heidi Hansen, of San Diego, and structural drawings by Cynthia A. Lewis, of Hayward, included extending the kitchen, adding a new

In dining room, brick fireplace has interesting moldings on wooden overmantel.

Professor of Italian Roberto Sangiorgi poses with bust.

child's bedroom and master bathroom upstairs, and a new forced-air heating system. Apart from the east-facing kitchen wall, nothing that remained of the original 1913 Ratcliff design was removed. Concrete-based terra-cotta tiles replaced the damaged clay tile roofing.

Poor-quality doors and moldings put in after the 1956 fire (presumably for financial reasons) were upgraded: the solid wood doors have brass handles. On the interior stairway, solid oak replaced the somewhat flimsy newel post, as well as the handrail and balusters. All interior molding was replaced, and all rooms now have ceiling molding.

New red oak flooring replaced badly damaged floors in the dining room, upstairs bedroom, and upstairs hallway. Elsewhere, existing ones were refinished. The kitchen and dining room floors have inlaid walnut borders in the red oak.

The kitchen was extended about 6 feet, providing a breakfast area with French doors; the attic above was also extended. Lynda Hastie notes: "We demolished the old kitchen with the exception of the brick fireplace [bread oven], which we could not bear to lose.... We had a 1920s Wedgewood stove remodeled and installed in the kitchen —what a beauty!" Old cabinets were replaced with maple ones. Oak flooring replaced linoleum.

On the second floor, the master bedroom and bath gained about 175 square feet including a generous walk-in closet. The bathroom includes a whirlpool tub and frameless glass shower; tiles were made in Valencia, Spain. Part of the new bath cantilevers 8 feet beyond the first-floor exterior wall; to support this expansion, the foundation below was rebuilt.

A new bathroom serves the two small bedrooms nearby, including the new child's bedroom built on the deck area from the Sangiorgis' remodel. On the first floor, the bedroom on the west end became a study.

The patio off the dining room was completely refurbished, including new low-voltage lighting and a watering system. On the living room wall facing the patio, Portuguese blue-and-white tiles form a charming wine scene. Off the kitchen, a 500-square-foot tiled patio is large enough for outdoor entertaining and barbecuing. And off the study is a redwood deck. The veranda wall on the front of the house now extends farther to the left, with steps up to the main floor. Metal handrails, formed by an ironsmith, run up the two flights of stairs at the entrance to the veranda.

This historic house on its remarkable property remains a fascinating reminder of the university's early days. ❋

In the kitchen, brick bread oven added by the Sangiorgis is now back in working order.

On living room wall facing the back patio, Portuguese tiles portray a monk enjoying a sip or two in a wine cellar.

SOURCES

Architectural drawings, Davis memorial article, and Wilson garden article. Collection of Trevor and Lynda Hastie.

Campbell, Douglas H. Papers, SC 22, Stanford University Archives (includes incoming correspondence from 1888–1953, only up through M).

Campbell, Douglas Houghton. "Professor Robert Edgar Allardice." *Stanford Illustrated Review*, 29 (June 1928): 464–465.

Davis, Bradley M., et al. "A Memorial of Douglas Houghton Campbell, 1859–1953." *The Asa Gray Bulletin* NS II, 2 (Spring 1953): 103–48.

Hastie, Lynda. Memos to authors (27 May and 3 June 1999).

Hastie, Trevor. Conversations and house tour with authors (summer 1998).

House files, 1040 Campus Drive. Two sheets for 1990 renovation; seven sheets for 1998 renovation. Stanford University Maps and Records.

Memorial Resolution: Robert C. Allardice (1862–1928). Stanford University Academic Council.

Memorial Resolution: Douglas H. Campbell (1859–1952). Stanford University Academic Council.

Photos of house details before the remodeling and addition (June 1998). Collection of Trevor and Lynda Hastie.

Post-fire reconstruction records, 1040 Campus Drive (1956). Stanford University Faculty Housing Office.

Ratcliff, Walter H., Jr. Construction specifications, 1040 Campus Drive. Stanford Planning Office Records, SC 123, Box 4C, Folder 14, Stanford University Archives.

"Ravaging Fire Destroys Home of Professor: Sangiorgi Was Away When Blaze Erupted." *The Stanford Daily* (30 January 1956).

Sangiorgi, Mrs. Silvana Laurelli, Rome Italy. Letter to David Weber (24 August 1998).

Wiggins, Ira L. "Douglas Houghton Campbell in the Classroom and on the Campus." *American Fern Journal* (July-September 1953): 102.

Wilson, Albert. "Douglas Houghton Campbell's Garden at Stanford University." Reprinted from *Journal of the California Horticultural Society* 14, no. 4 (1953): 142–152.

PHOTOS

Allardice and Campbell, Stanford Archives; Allardice (seated), Hastie collection; Sangiorgi, Stanford News Service; tile and kitchen, David Weber; all others, Margaret McKinnon.

1050 Campus Drive

(526 Mayfield, 526 Campus Drive)

BYRON FEIG

1925~Tudor period style

ARCHITECT	OWNERS
Unknown; perhaps Charles K. Sumner	Briggs—Wolf/Gates

BY HILL GATES

This stucco house, full of architectural surprises, entices visitors indoors to explore hidden nooks, then draws them out again to enjoy the garden on the sloping grounds. What is known of the house's history comes largely from the structure itself, the many small objects left behind, and what artifacts and letters have passed down to its current owners.

Original records of designer, builder, and cost have been lost. According to the Santa Clara County assessor's records, 1925 was the year of its construction, but its designer is unknown. The house's similarities in style and materials to nearby houses, especially 536 and 562 Gerona, suggest that the architect was the locally well-known Charles K. Sumner. The first owners were William Dinsmore Briggs and his wife, Ethel Twitchell Briggs. The original address was 526 Mayfield, later changed to 526 Campus Drive, and more recently to its present numbering.

The 3,500-square-foot house, which faces north onto Campus Drive, has a 27-foot-long brick-floored entry hall paneled in mahogany-stained redwood, which was also used in the living room's end walls, the stairway, and the second-story hall.

To the right is the Craftsman-style living room, unchanged today except for furnishings. This 18- by 36-foot great room has dark-stained oak floors and buff-colored stucco on the barrel-vaulted ceiling. The fireplace, on the west wall, is framed by its original tiles patterned with vines and grape clusters. On each side are built-in cupboards with leaded-glass doors. Floor-to-ceiling redwood bookshelves fill the east wall, and Roman-arched bookshelves and recessed windows cover the north wall. The south wall, which looks out to the garden, has more shelves, an alcove, and a door to a 14-foot-square sunroom.

At the opposite end of the entry hall is the 14- by 18-foot dining room with recessed windows and brick floor. The fireplace, on the north wall, has its original patterned tile. Off this room are the kitchen, breakfast room, and pantry as well as a small utility room. In 1987, Arthur Wolf removed a wall that divided the original kitchen, creating space for several pieces of handsome Chinese furniture, now used to store kitchen and dining supplies.

Time has brought few other changes. The beautiful green-tiled sunporch was probably an afterthought, and its green-painted interior remained from Ethel Briggs's time until the Wolfs whitewashed it.

From the entry hall, the paneled staircase leads to the second-floor hall. Off it are a master bedroom, bath, a trunk room, and another bedroom that serves as a study and guest room and contains an ornate antique Chinese wedding bed. Floors on this story are softwood, most likely fir.

Probably the house's most surprising feature is concealed behind an unobtrusive arched door under the staircase. Instead of just a closet beyond the door, as one might expect, there is a suite of south-facing rooms adjacent to the kitchen and living room but not connected to them. It includes a study, bath, and a room Mrs. Briggs used as a bedroom when she could no longer climb the stairs.

Glassed-in sunporch off living room extends into back garden.

Under the staircase, "secret" door reveals a suite of rooms including study, bath, and bedroom.

Life in this house was more gracious and undoubtedly more socially complex under its first owners than under the present ones. Stanford wives surely did housework, but an expectation of help was built in to the very fabric of the house. A pretty little above-garage apartment is original, as is the servants' toilet in the basement. A bell embedded in the dining room floor once summoned a server. The glassed-in, but gloomy, northeast back porch has electrical outlets positioned perfectly for ironing clothes just up from the basement laundry. No driveway reaches the back door, so all supplies were, and still are, carried to the kitchen along a 30-yard-long, walled-off uphill path, and then up the back stairs.

The garden on the south side of the house is terraced with lawn and flowers, as well as large pine, oak, and redwood trees. A stand of bamboo covers the southwest corner and reflects the current owners' love of China. Handsome bits of sandstone rubble from the 1906 earthquake, souvenirs of earlier Stanford history, are found in small retaining walls and in paths.

In 1969, Arthur and Margery Wolf bought the house from the estate of Ethel Briggs.

Although the house had enough shelving to accommodate the Wolfs' young library, by 1986 the bibliophilic overflow had become unmanageable, so a carpenter added about 225 linear feet of bookshelves along with numerous file cupboards and cabinets. These now dominate two or more downstairs rooms and one upstairs. The dining room, one of the bedrooms, and the bathroom were spared, and the kitchen held steady at its original 15 feet of shelves. When Hill Gates joined Arthur Wolf at the residence, they needed all these shelves and more.

The 1989 Loma Prieta earthquake irreparably cracked the dining room fireplace and toppled a long stucco wall that linked the house to the garage. After a decade of delay, Wolf and Gates built a perfect replacement wall, finished with three coats of stucco. The house stands today largely as it was built.

Was the garden plan inspired by Professor or Mrs. Briggs? Or by the unknown architect or an undiscovered landscaper? Judging by the beauty of the back garden, where the original rock terraces remain, someone deserves great credit for gracious use of the cool, north-facing hillside. Much else, however, has changed in the garden. The prolonged drought of the late 1980s coincided with the years of Gates's and Wolf's frequent absences for fieldwork in China, and resident tenants' unfamiliarity with the demands of California's dry summers. A dozen trees and most of the front lawn died, leaving the property circled

Three views of the living room show rich paneling, multiple bookcases, arched ceiling, and original ceiling lights. Fireplace has original tiles and brass fender seats, and glass-doored bookcases set into wall on each side. Near the opposite end (above), glass door opens to sunporch.

with resilient redwoods and oaks.

More water-wise now, the owners have filled in the new, sunny spaces with fruit trees and a meadow. Wolf resculpted parts of the back garden to improve drainage after a series of wet-basement years, a paradoxical consequence of drought. His new retaining wall of old Stanford sandstone, a true Great Wall of China in labor and design, merges seamlessly with the Briggses' gentle diagonals and playful perspectives.

By benign neglect, the house escaped the remodeling trends of the 1950s and '60s and, even worse, the 1980s. Today, with their two cats, and their priceless collection of anthropology slides entombed in the safe built for Professor Briggs's notes, Arthur Wolf and Hill Gates find it a dwelling as well fitted to them as to the couple who built it. Together, they wish it a plainly preserved future when they, in turn, pass it on to another small, bookish household.

The Owners

~William Dinsmore Briggs~

Briggs, born in Ohio in 1876, earned his bachelor's degree in English at Stanford in 1896. After some time at Johns Hopkins University, he received his Ph.D. from Harvard in 1900. He taught at the University of Vermont and Western Reserve University before returning to Stanford in 1906 as an assistant professor of English; he was a renowned teacher and an authority on the playwrights and poets Christopher Marlowe and Ben Jonson. From 1925 until his death, in 1941, he served as head of the English Department.

English professor William Briggs filled his house with books.

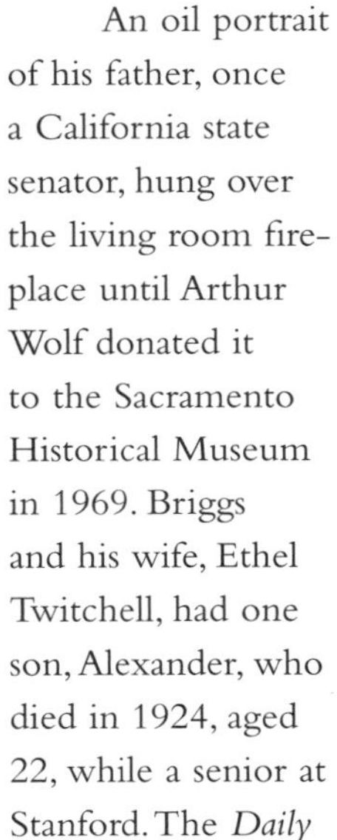

An oil portrait of his father, once a California state senator, hung over the living room fireplace until Arthur Wolf donated it to the Sacramento Historical Museum in 1969. Briggs and his wife, Ethel Twitchell, had one son, Alexander, who died in 1924, aged 22, while a senior at Stanford. The *Daily Palo Alto Times* wrote: "A glass containing a solution of cyanide of potassium, found near him and believed to have been used in the course of chemical experimentation, is supposed to have been the cause of death." His parents found the body when they returned home to Palo Alto from San Francisco. An inquest returned a verdict that the young man had met his death by "swallowing cyanide, self-administered and accidentally."

Professor Briggs was a scholar's scholar, as his house so plainly attests. The seemingly endless bookshelves in the living room were hardly enough, but Professor Briggs sacrificed some shelving space to insert a 4- by 6-foot safe in the south wall for his note cards.

Apparently, the house's living room and Briggs's Stanford English Department office did not satisfy his desire to live surrounded by books. Sixty yards south of the house's main entrance, he built a large cottage as his study, the interior of which was encircled by bookshelves. In the 1960s or before, the cottage was sold as a separate property, now 1060 Campus Drive. The stone path that links the sunporch door to this retreat is now impassable, overgrown with pink 'Climbing Cécile Brunner' roses and the neighbor's mottled bamboo.

Briggs was honored, posthumously, by the dedication of the English Department's library to him in 1942; it is still known as the Briggs Room. In honor of the dedication, two poems were written, one by his colleague Yvor Winters titled "For the Opening of the William Dinsmore Briggs Room." It reads:

> Because our Being grows in mind,
> And evil in imperfect thought,
> And passion running undefined
> May ruin what the masters taught;
>
> Within the edge of war we meet
> To dedicate this room to one
> Who made his wisdom more complete
> Than any save the great have done;
>
> That in this room, men yet may reach,
> By labor and wit's sullen shock,
> The final certitude of speech
> Which Hell itself cannot unlock.

Ethel Briggs's collection of opera scores, the etchings and watercolors from her European travels, and a packet of letters from her only child tell us of a cultivated woman. Her piles of cocktail-sized Haviland china plates and Royal Worcester bouillon cups suggest her presence as a hostess.

A technically unsophisticated, yet charming, oil portrait of Ethel, perhaps in her 30s, was passed down with the house. In 1969, she died in a Menlo Park rest home.

~ARTHUR WOLF~

The David and Lucile Packard Professor in Human Biology was born in 1932 in Santa Rosa, California, the son of a sharecropper father and dairywoman mother. He supported himself through Santa Rosa Junior College by summer mining and logging until he was awarded a Telluride Fellowship to Cornell University in 1952. Initially studying English literature, he switched subjects, receiving a Ph.D. in psychological anthropology in 1963.

A year each at the London School of Economics and All Souls College, Oxford, provided new perspectives, and lengthy fieldwork in Taiwan supplied abundant evidence for a lifetime career in the branch of anthropology most concerned with unraveling the interplay of biology and culture in human affairs. For 30 years, he has been amassing a vast archive of information about early 20th-century Taiwan households. This work and other studies in comparative Taiwan/Dutch demography continue while he teaches in Anthropological Sciences.

Arthur Wolf's second wife, Hill Gates, is a graduate of Radcliffe College with a Ph.D. in anthropology from the University of Michigan (1973). She was born in 1942 in Canada and taught for 20 years at Central Michigan University, combining pedagogy with fieldwork in Taiwan and China. Her three books display her interests in the Chinese world and the ways in which Westerners attempt to understand it. After Gates and Wolf were married, in 1990, she was a lecturer in anthropology at Stanford for 10 years. Now, in addition to her professional work, she is a part-time earth mother for a stream of delightful Chinese and Dutch anthropologists, demographers, and historians.

As diversions from academic life, Wolf and Gates maintain the Wolf family property in northern Sonoma County. On the working lamb, venison, wild pork, turkey, and wildflower ranch, they are building a second house, cutting the lumber and doing the work themselves. ❋

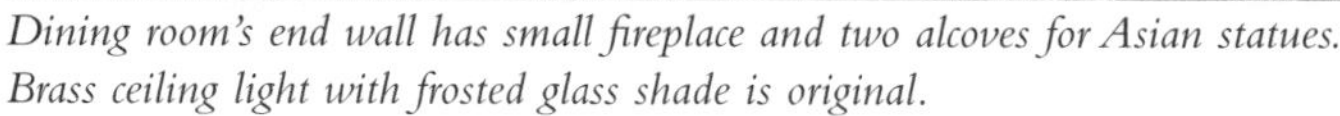

Dining room's end wall has small fireplace and two alcoves for Asian statues. Brass ceiling light with frosted glass shade is original.

SOURCES

Bourland, Benjamin P. Correspondence (8 November 1908 to 22 July 1911). Collection of Arthur Wolf.

Carnochan, W. B., "English at Stanford 1891–2000: A Brief History." *Sandstone & Tile* (Stanford Historical Society) 26, no.1 (Winter/Spring 2002).

"Alex Briggs Killed by Poison Fluid" [obit]. *Daily Palo Alto Times* (21 February 1924).

"Ethel Briggs" [obit]. *Palo Alto Times* (2 May 1969).

"Poems for Dedication of Briggs Room." *New Mexico Quarterly Review* 12, no. 1 (February 1942).

"William Briggs" [obit]. *Palo Alto Times* (17 February 1941).

PHOTOS

Briggs, Stanford Archives; all others, Leni Hazlett.

743 Cooksey Lane

BYRON FEIG

1917 ~ California cottage style

DESIGNER/CONTRACTOR	OWNERS
George Wilbert Mosher	Brown—Schultz —Leavitt —Bankman/Fried

BY JOHN HARBAUGH AND MARIAN LEIB ADAMS

This one-story house is an example of the California cottage style popular from about 1910 until the late 1920s. Though many original features have disappeared in extensive remodeling over the years, triangular wooden roof brackets supporting the wide eaves, and cedar shingles (now painted taupe) on the exterior walls remain. Inside, some small-paned windows also remain, as does a china cabinet in the dining room.

The house was designed for Harold C. Brown by George Wilbert Mosher, who apparently also served as its contractor. Mosher's reputation was principally that of a contractor, and he is best known for the Squire House, the imposing white mansion at 900 University Avenue, Palo Alto, built in 1904. In 1911, he also purchased land on the 700 block of Waverley Street, Palo Alto, with John Dudfield. In the next seven years, they built eight Craftsman-style bungalows, all of which remain today.

The 2,500-square-foot house faces west, approached along a path through a cottage garden. The path, stairs, and porch floor are surfaced with gray slate with a diamond-shaped inset pattern. Of the extensive internal and external modifications, the most notable from the street is the flat-roofed sunroom addition, which occupies much of the former front porch.

The house has two wings connected by an entrance hall. The wing to the left includes a large, airy living room, 21 by 24 feet, as well as a dining room, powder room, laundry room, and modern kitchen. To the left off the hall is a sunroom, with a library–family room straight ahead. The sleeping wing to the right of the front entrance includes three bedrooms and a study.

A dramatic feature in the living room is the fireplace refaced with slate in a herringbone pattern with diamond insets similar to stonework in the entry porch. The slate's multicolored earth tones suggest deserts of the Southwest. Opposite the fireplace, a large single-pane window has replaced an original small-paned one. The other windows are original—double-hung and multipaned. On the north wall, two recessed windows have built-in window seats. French doors on the south wall lead to the front porch. Walls are painted cream with white trim.

The dining room retains a small built-in china cabinet and wainscoting (up to 5 feet), which has been painted white. The original brick fireplace, which shares a chimney with the living room one, has also been painted white. Original double-hung windows open on the north wall. Doors lead to the kitchen, the entry hall, and the living room, allowing these spaces to flow together while maintaining their separateness. Oak floors in the living and dining rooms enhance the continuity.

Next to the dining room is a powder room. It opens to the hall, which leads through the laundry room and into the tile-floored kitchen. The kitchen, which has been remodeled several times, opens onto a deck that runs the length of the back of the house and offers opportunities for outdoor dining. The library–family room, with a door off the entry hall, also opens to the deck. It has another patterned slate fireplace, in blue-green tones also evoking the Southwest. Bookshelves frame the fireplace.

In the bedroom wing, the master bedroom has been enlarged over the years and now has French doors to the deck and a hot tub. In 1966 a swimming pool and a large rear deck were added; the deck was replaced in 2003.

The entrance hall once had a curious feature. Three doors faced the front door. One led to the family room, and the other two led nowhere, with a solid wall behind them. Early house plans solve the mystery. The original house was designed with two closets opening to the entrance hall; between them, the third door went into a 10- by 14-foot study. At some point, a bedroom adjacent to the study was eliminated, and the combined space became the 14- by 18-foot library–family room. The closets were removed but not the doors. The Leavitts, finding this anomaly, had the door openings studded over and made part of the surrounding wall.

Shingled cottage, with sunroom and front entry between two wings, is surrounded by cottage garden and wooden fence.

Thoroughly modern touch: original brick of the dining room fireplace has been painted white.

Also in the original house plans, a maid's room and bath were next to the kitchen. There were three sleeping porches, two off the master bedroom (on each side of the bath) and one on the southwest corner of the house. During the Leavitts' tenure, the master bedroom porches were converted to a reading room and an outdoor deck. The maid's room became the powder room and laundry room, and a second closet became part of the powder room.

The Designer and Builder

~GEORGE WILBERT MOSHER~

Mosher was born in Nova Scotia in 1863. At 14 he began to work in the shipbuilding trade on the East Coast, and in 1885 he came west with his brother and a friend to work for the Southern Pacific Railroad. Returning to Nova Scotia in 1887, he married Helen McNealy, and they then settled in Santa Cruz.

In 1891, he moved to Palo Alto to work at Stanford and was the first builder and contractor in town, as well as member of the first Palo Alto city council, in 1909. He built Manzanita Hall at Stanford and 300 houses in Palo Alto, costing $1,000 to $5,000 each.

Throughout his career, he took an interest in the establishment of societies that aided builders and the building industry. According to *History of State of California and Biographical Records of the Coast Counties,* Mosher "felt that building was an art and his work was known for substantiality, appropriateness, connection with surroundings and artistic effects. He was a master workman, understanding every facet of his interesting and constantly improving occupation."

Mosher and his wife had one child, Allene. He retired in 1937 and died two years later at his home on Webster Street in Palo Alto.

The Owners

~HAROLD CHAPMAN BROWN~

The first owner, an expert on mathematical philosophy and the philosophy of language, was born in Springfield, Massachusetts, in 1879. Brown graduated from Williams College in 1901, and received a Ph.D. from Harvard in 1905. Before joining Stanford's Philosophy Department in 1914, Brown was an instructor at Columbia University. He actively supported labor and cooperative movements and the American Civil Liberties Union. When the United States entered World War I, in 1917, he took leave to serve as a field director for the American Red Cross at nearby Camp Fremont. He returned to Stanford after the war and continued to teach, including his popular aesthetics course, which was enhanced by his love of music. He served as executive head of the department until illness forced him to take early retirement about six months before his death, in 1943.

~EDWIN WILLIAM SCHULTZ~

In 1926, Professor Brown sold the house to Dr. Schultz, who had joined the faculty of Stanford's School of Medicine in 1920, three years after he had received his M.D. from Johns Hopkins University. Dr. Schultz was born in Lomira, Wisconsin, in 1888. After undergraduate studies at Winona College of Agriculture in Indiana (B.S.A., 1913) and at Michigan (A.B., 1914), he married Anna Francel Roberts that year.

During World War I, he served in the U.S. Army Medical Corps, and was chief of the laboratory at one of the 33rd Division's base hospitals in France. At Stanford, he served as a professor and long-time chair in the Department of Bacteriology and Experimental Pathology, later renamed the Department of Medical Microbiology. A charter Guggenheim Fellow in 1925, Schultz studied in Egypt and Paris, where he acquired the interest in viruses that shaped his career. He taught both on the Palo Alto campus and at the Medical School in San Francisco. He played a major role in the 1959 relocation of the Medical School to campus.

After he retired, in 1953, Schultz and his wife lived for seven years in Jakarta, Indonesia, where he directed a project to reconstruct the curriculum at the University of Indonesia Medical School. The Schultzes returned to the house on Cooksey Lane until they sold it to Harold and Gloria Leavitt in 1966. Edwin Schultz died in 1971. Schultz Auditorium in the old Anatomy Building was named in his honor.

Harold Chapman Brown

Harold Leavitt

~Harold J. Leavitt~

Leavitt was born in Lynn, Massachusetts, in 1922. He earned a bachelor's degree from Harvard in 1943 and a master's in psychology from Brown University in 1944. He then served two years with the U.S. Navy as a personnel research officer at the Marine Corps' Medical Field Research Laboratory at Camp Lejeune, North Carolina.

Returning to civilian life in 1946, Leavitt spent the next three years at M.I.T., earning a Ph.D. in industrial relations. He taught psychology at Rensselaer Polytechnic Institute, then organizational behavior at the University of Chicago and Carnegie Institute of Technology. In 1966, he joined Stanford's Graduate School of Business as professor of organizational behavior. The house on Cooksey Lane became home to the Leavitts and their three children.

Leavitt had met his future wife, Gloria Rosenthal, while he was an undergraduate. During World War II, while he was at Brown, she became a first-class welder at the Walsh-Kaiser shipyard in Providence, Rhode Island, helping to build corvettes for the British Royal Navy.

Leavitt relates that the family was surprised when they arrived at the house. They had come from the East, where three years earlier they had built a contemporary redwood house near Pittsburgh, Pennsylvania. They had not envisioned a cottage with a spread-out floor plan and a sleeping porch. With its gas water heater in the kitchen and its small bedrooms, the house was something of a shock. However, with major modifications and embellishments, including removal of the two doors that led nowhere, the Leavitts gradually came to love their house.

From the outset, the family found the garden to be a grand affair. It spanned nearly an acre, and was filled with tall redwood trees and a magnificent stone fireplace that had been built by the Schultz sons. The garden provided a splendid place for ceremonies marking important events, and for receptions and parties.

In 1985, Gloria Leavitt died. Several years later, Harold Leavitt married Jean Lipman-Blumen, a fellow at the Center for Advanced Studies in the Behavioral Sciences and later a faculty member at the Peter Drucker School of Business in Claremont. They were married in the Cooksey Lane garden. In 1987, Harold Leavitt retired from Stanford, and he and his wife moved to Pasadena.

~Joseph Bankman and Barbara Fried~

Since 1991, Bankman and Fried, both professors in the Stanford Law School, have owned the house. Bankman, born in 1955 in Moline, Illinois, graduated from UC Berkeley in 1977 and from Yale Law School in 1980. Until 1984, he was a member of the law firm of Tuttle and Taylor in Los Angeles, then professor at the University of Southern California Law School. An expert on tax law, he came to Stanford in 1989.

Barbara Fried, born in 1951 in New York City, is an expert on tax law and political theory. She earned bachelor's and master's degrees from Harvard in 1977 and 1980, respectively. After receiving her law degree from Harvard in 1983, she spent a year as a law clerk on the Second Circuit Court of Appeals, then joined the New York City law firm of Paul Weiss Rifkind Wharton & Garrison. She came to Stanford in 1987. She is an amateur cellist and plays in a local string quartet.

The house is the scene of much merriment for friends and neighbors of the Bankman-Fried household, including their two sons. They frequently arrange gatherings that include games and contests. ❋

SOURCES

Brown, Harold Chapman [biographical information]: *Stanford University Alumni Directory* (1955).

Fried, Barbara: interview with John Harbaugh (February 2003).

"George Wilbert Mosher" [article]. *Palo Alto Times* (16 February 1894).

"George Wilbert Mosher" [obit]. *Palo Alto Times* (6 May 1939).

History of State of California and Biographical Record of the Coast Counties. Chicago: The Chapman Publishing Company (1904).

Leavitt, Harold: e-mail correspondence with John Harbaugh (ca. 1998).

Memorial resolution: Harold Brown (1879–1943). Stanford University Academic Council.

Memorial resolution: Edwin Schultz (1888–1971). Stanford University Academic Council.

Schultz, Edwin W. [biographical information]: *Stanford University Alumni Directory* (1955).

PHOTOS

Brown, Kee Coleman/Stanford News Service; Leavitt, Graduate School of Business; all others, Leni Hazlett.

740 Santa Ynez Street

(9 Aibonito, 9 Cabrillo, 740 Cabrillo)

BYRON FEIG

By Marian Leib Adams

This two-story shingled house was designed in 1909 in the Craftsman style with an Asian influence by Oakland architect A.W. Smith. The house is square, with a pitched roof that curves up slightly at the lower edges.

1909 ~ Craftsman style

ARCHITECT	OWNERS
A. W. Smith	Bassett—Smith—Adams

The house, with approximately 3,000 square feet plus a basement and attic, is built on a north-south axis with the front entrance facing south onto Santa Ynez. Large double-hung windows allow in much natural light. From the outside, they appear almost randomly placed, but this asymmetry was common in the Craftsman style, where the house was designed from the inside out, and rooms were laid out for function rather than for visual symmetry.

Another hallmark of the Craftsman style is the use of local building materials and, in this case, the choice of redwood for structural beams, detailing, and exterior shingles.

At the front of the house, stairs, originally of wood but now of brick, lead to a porch whose supporting beams form two *torii* shapes. This design, derived from gates (torii) to Japanese temples, continues throughout the house in various subtle forms: in the first-floor window and door frames, shelf supports, and living room mantel.

Inside the front door, a spacious front hall includes a closet under the open staircase that climbs across the back of the hall; a window seat in the hall also serves as a storage locker. Pocket doors lead to the living room on the left and the formal dining room on the right.

In the 15- by 21-foot living room, the large clinker-brick fireplace has a raised hearth; the mantel is a massive redwood beam supported on bricks in the torii form. The fireplace dominates the room and draws visitors to its warmth. Built-in shelves at one end and a window seat at the other, both included in the original plan, remain. In the living room, as in much of the house, original light fixtures are still in use.

A small room off the back of the living room, originally a den, is now the dining room. Its original built-in shelves and window seat have been removed.

Next to this room is the kitchen with a separate utility area, which has screened sliding windows and a cool closet vented to the outside. A door leads to a back porch, and wooden stairs descend to the driveway. Off the utility area, a small bathroom still has its original stone tile floor. In the kitchen are two pantry closets, one of which has screened shelves and a vent that can be opened to the basement's cooler temperatures.

To the right of the entry, the former dining room is now a music and play room. It has a coved ceiling and display shelves above the 5-foot redwood wainscoting. Two torii forms support a built-in glass-fronted china cabinet.

Most floors in the house are of white oak. The original fir floors in the kitchen have been restored; utility room floors are protected with linoleum. The interior trim is redwood, stained dark downstairs but mostly in its natural tone upstairs.

Originally the upstairs included four bedrooms, a screened sleeping porch, a bathroom with a tub, and a trunk closet with a ladder to a full attic; the closet is now a second bathroom. The master bedroom has two closets, one of which doubles as a passageway from the bedroom to the bathroom. One of the bedrooms has a sink, while another with built-in shelves can be used as a study. A third bedroom with shelves on all four walls serves as a library. The sleeping porch is also a study. A long hall, connecting the upstairs rooms, leads to a small balcony porch over the living room, on the west side of the house.

Because of the lot's slope toward the back, the basement expands from a crawl space on the front of the house to a full story on the back, which includes a one-room

Two elevations show south-facing front of house (left) with steps up to front porch, and east-facing side (right) with end of front porch at left and back deck off dining room. Lot's slope toward the back is evident in side view.

ELENA ANGOLOTI

apartment. This may have been built as servants' quarters; in later years, it was occasionally rented to students.

In the garden are a variety of trees, including plums, guava, pine, redwood, and six large oaks. Informal garden beds were originally laid out on the hillside at the back, with front, side, and back lawns. Today, flower beds have replaced the lawns.

The Architect

~A. W. Smith~

The house's designer, Alfred William Smith (1860–1933), came to California as a child and lived the rest of his life in Oakland, where he practiced for 40 years as a contractor and architect. He designed hundreds of houses and commercial buildings in the East Bay, many of which are still occupied.

Best known for his Craftsman- and shingle-style houses, Smith also designed in other styles. He was known, according to a report on unreinforced masonry buildings in Oakland from 1850 to 1948, for his "exuberant use of the geometric and colorful qualities of brick, mortar, tile and glass." Houses he designed in Berkeley and Oakland are staples on East Bay historic house tours.

Smith published frequently in *The Architect and Engineer,* in which he outlined his admiration of the Craftsman philosophy that dominated most of his designs. On the Stanford campus, he designed at least one other house (at 739 Santa Ynez) and three student residences: Haus Mitteleuropa, 620 Mayfield (1910); Kairos, 586 Mayfield (1911); and Phi Kappa Psi, 592 Mayfield (1911). The Palo Alto Historical Association attributes to him the design of several houses in the city: 425 Embarcadero, 360 Leland, 601 Melville, and 1221 Waverley.

The Owners

~Lee Emerson Bassett~

On November 30, 1908, Bassett, a professor of English, applied to the Board of Trustees for a 10-year lease for the lot at the northwest corner of Cooksey Lane and Aibonito Avenue (now Santa Ynez Street). He also applied for a loan of $2,500 to complete and pay for a house, and requested "the privilege of erecting a small barn and of keeping a driving horse on the property." The estimated cost of the house was $4,000; he received the lease on December 7, 1908.

In early January 1909, Bassett and his wife, Florence Jackson Bassett, traveled to Oakland to meet with the architect. They'd been directed to him by their neighbors John Ezra McDowell, academic and alumni secretary, and his wife, Alice Nagel McDowell, who lived across the street at 739 Santa Ynez and for whom Smith had also designed a house. By January 30, the Bassetts had the house plans, which they put out for bid to four contractors, ultimately deciding on B. J. Bean, a Palo Alto builder, whose bid was $4,350.

Excavation for the foundation began in March but was somewhat impeded, Bassett wrote in his journal, by

In backyard "tractor park," star is a single-cylinder gas-powered road roller from about 1910.

Lee Emerson Bassett, professor of English and the house's first owner, did much of the finishing detail on the house.

the "mucky nature of the soil—adobe." But construction progressed rapidly and by the end of the month the house was nearly enclosed and ready for shingling. Professor Bassett's journal reveals several adjustments to the original plan and conflicts with the builder, as changes were made and costs exceeded the budget. However, the Bassetts were intrigued by their project, frequently visiting the site to supervise the work and to plan and plant the garden that would include 14 fruit trees as well as coast live oak and valley oak seedlings, now magnificent mature trees.

When the internal lath work began, Professor Bassett started working at the house on weekends and in the evenings, sometimes with the help of his friend and neighbor, education professor Ellwood P. Cubberley. Bassett enjoyed woodworking and took great care in the detailing of his house.

On June 26, the Bassetts moved into their new home, enjoying a supper prepared by their neighbors the McDowells. The house was approved by the builder on June 28, a formality required by the university to advance the "acceptance" (loan) payment, and the Bassetts settled into a routine. Professor Bassett attended to academics in the mornings and finished the detail work on the house in the afternoons. Only a month later, on July 28, the Bassetts' first son, William Meredith, was born at home.

At the back of the lot, Professor Bassett built his small barn, which was later converted to a garage and workshop. Because of the lot's slope, rubble from the 1906 earthquake was used in an attempt to level the ground. Evidence of sandstone and mosaic fragments from the church façade can still be found embedded in the garden paths.

Lee Emerson Bassett was born in Salem, Wisconsin, in 1872. After graduating from Stanford in 1901, he was appointed instructor in English, specializing in the oral interpretation of English literature. In 1903, he married Florence Jackson, a teacher, in San Francisco. Their elder son, William, entered the U.S. Navy in 1941 and was lost at sea in 1944. Their second son, David Lee, born in 1913, earned his bachelor's degree in 1934 and his medical degree in 1939 from Stanford. He went on to a distinguished career as professor of anatomy at Stanford Medical School and later as head of the Division of Gross Anatomy at the University of Washington. He and his wife, Lucile, had four children who grew up playing in their grandparents' garden.

Professor Bassett's career at Stanford follows the development of the speech and drama program. When he was appointed to the faculty in 1901, speech and elocution were not widely accepted as university courses, although debate and drama were popular extracurricular activities. As a senior, Bassett had been asked by President David Starr Jordan to assist Stanford's intercollegiate debating team and help with

Craftsman details abound in the house: in living room, clinker-brick fireplace with mantel made from a redwood beam, original wall fixtures, redwood-framed windows, seating alcove at one end (hung with Christmas decorations).

student drama productions. Of the many early plays he directed with the English Club, one—the 1903 production of *The Knight of the Burning Pestle*—has been twice revived by the Stanford Drama Department, once as the 50th-anniversary commemorative production in Bassett's honor in 1953, and again in 2003.

For more than 10 years, Bassett taught all the speech classes (he was the only teacher) and coached an award-winning debate team, struggling to keep the speech program alive. However, during World War I, the need for officers who could give orders clearly and concisely reached American universities. Speech, as an undergraduate subject, found new support.

In 1919, Bassett was promoted to full professor and named executive head of the Division of Public Speaking in the Department of English. Meanwhile, student interest in drama had grown rapidly, and with completion of Memorial Hall in 1937, drama was linked with public speaking to form the new Department of Speech and Drama. Bassett was its chair in the new but short-lived School of Fine Arts. He retired the following year. When the School of Humanities was organized in 1941, Speech and Drama was the largest of the fine arts units folded into the new school.

During his years at Stanford, Bassett stressed the scholarly underpinnings of the study of oral English literature and dramatic literature, and published many articles and two books. In 1926, he published the *Handbook of Oral Reading,* with a foreword by President Jordan, his long-time supporter, who emphasized the need for students to "think on their feet and to speak clearly honestly and effectively."

Over the years, Bassett took an active part in regional and national professional organizations. He also taught at Northwestern and the universities of Colorado, Washington, and Hawaii. Serving as president of the Western Speech Association and the Speech Association of America, he continued his 20-year-long interest in the Palo Alto Toastmasters' Club (which was renamed the Lee Emerson Bassett Chapter in his honor).

The Bassetts celebrated their 50th wedding anniversary at the house in 1953. Florence Bassett died the following year. In 1955, Professor Bassett sold the house to Dr. Jay Ward Smith for $18,000 and moved to a small house in Palo Alto to be closer to his son and his family. Professor Bassett died in 1959.

~Jay Ward Smith~

Dr. Smith, who was born in 1918 in Ottawa, Kansas, earned his bachelor's degree in basic medical sciences in 1940 and his medical degree in 1944, both from Stanford. An internist specializing in infectious diseases at the Stanford Medical School, Smith also served on the dean's staff, planning the 1959 move of the school's faculty and laboratories from San Francisco to the home campus. The process was not easy, as there were many issues to resolve and much resistance to the move from the teaching and clinical faculties. After three years of almost nonstop meetings and controversy, Dr. Smith left the university in 1958 to enter private practice

Pedal-powered jigsaw (1875), which belonged to Jim Adams's grandfather, is among the owners' many collections.

Glass-fronted china cabinet in former dining room (now music and play room) is supported by Japanese torii at each end, a motif also used elsewhere.

in Menlo Park, although he continued to live in the house until 1971.

During the 16 years that Dr. Smith and his wife, Barbara, and their three children lived at the house, they made few structural changes. Instead, they built several outdoor structures, which no longer remain. Most memorable was the tree house in an oak at the northern fence line, which was a favorite meeting place for Frank Smith and his friends in the late 1960s. The tree still has traces of the Day-Glo paint popular in that era. Frank and his father built another tree house, high in an oak at the northwest corner of the property. Frank also is responsible for the mosaic fragments embedded in the garden path near the lower deck. The origin of the fragments is not known, but is likely the result of discreet scavenging some time after the 1906 earthquake, perhaps brought when the ground was leveled for construction of Bassett's barn.

~James L. Adams~

In 1971, Adams bought the house for $53,000, and moved there with his wife, Gretchen, and their sons, Robert and Daniel. They made few changes to the house except to paint the post–World War II pastel walls a consistent "Navajo" white. Professor Adams, a carpenter and builder by avocation, renovated the kitchen, adding cupboards and a tile counter around the sink. During this time, the family began a collection of farm equipment that has become a centerpiece of the Cooksey Lane side of the lot. They acquired their first tractor, an Oliver, which both Adams boys learned to drive.

James Adams was born on March 6, 1934, in Rialto, California, in his family's home amid an orange grove his grandparents had planted in the early 1900s. He earned engineering degrees from California Institute of Technology and Stanford, and studied art for a year at UCLA. From the Jet Propulsion Laboratory in Pasadena, he was recruited to teach in the Design Division of Stanford's Mechanical Engineering Department. In his 35 years at Stanford, Adams chaired various programs in engineering and the Program in Values, Technology, Science and Society. A popular teacher, he was recipient of several teaching awards, the Lloyd W. Dinkelspiel Award for Outstanding Service to Undergraduate Education, and the first Richard W. Lyman Award for Alumni Service.

After a divorce and living elsewhere, Adams returned to 740 Santa Ynez in 1981 with his second wife, Marian Leib Adams. She was born in 1942 and is a fourth-generation Californian. Her great-grandfather, Samuel Franklin Leib, a prominent San Jose attorney and judge, was a legal advisor to Governor and Mrs. Leland Stanford and a member of the university's original Board of Trustees; on Jane Stanford's death, in 1905, he became president of the board. Marian Adams worked at the Stanford Alumni Association for 24 years, 16 of them as director of continuing education. In 1993, she resigned to establish a consultancy in continuing education.

Her two children, Samuel and Elizabeth Player, along with Adams's son Daniel, occupied three upstairs bedrooms at the house, while Robert Adams, then an undergraduate at Stanford, camped on a small upstairs porch or in the student room in the basement when home on holidays. The upstairs storage closet was converted to a bathroom for the children.

Now the Adams and Player offspring are all out of the nest, their bedrooms and the sleeping porch have become a library, an extra bedroom, and studies for their parents, who have both retired.

From the front entrance, staircase has old-growth redwood newel and banister. Three lower stairs are oak; others are carpeted.

Although the house has gone through many changes in the last 20 years, all of them remain true to the original Craftsman-style design. A deck off the dining room extends over a carport for two vehicles and offers views of the garden. Another deck, built on the northern property line under a large oak tree, replaced an earlier one that was crushed by a falling branch during a storm.

The detached garage now contains a metal and woodworking shop for Jim and an orchid house for Marian. The rose garden, planted in memory of William Bassett by his mother, still has a few of her old-fashioned rose plants along with more than 40 new hybrids. An eclectic collection of outdoor sculpture and found objects adds contrast to the planted landscape. On a portion of the back garden, the collection of farm machinery has expanded from the original Oliver tractor to what the Adamses call a "tractor park." A smaller "park" has been added on the house's west side.

The plywood-floored attic now serves as prime storage space. The basement is also used for storage and has a workshop for Jim and a darkroom that doubles as a small wine cellar. The basement apartment also serves as storage space and, occasionally, a guest room. Both Adamses are collectors, and they have built many shelves throughout the house for books, collectibles, and *objets d'art et de technologie.* During the Christmas holidays, Nativities and tree ornaments from all over the world cover every inch of available space downstairs.

The house sustained some damage during the 1989 Loma Prieta earthquake, but fortunately it had been bolted to the foundation a few years before. The fireplace chimney and the long-unused chimney for the original kitchen woodstove collapsed, and plaster fell from several walls in the downstairs rooms. The plaster has been replaced with plywood and wallboard, and the fireplace chimney has been made more earthquake resistant, with an industrial smokestack and spark arrester that are lighter in weight than the

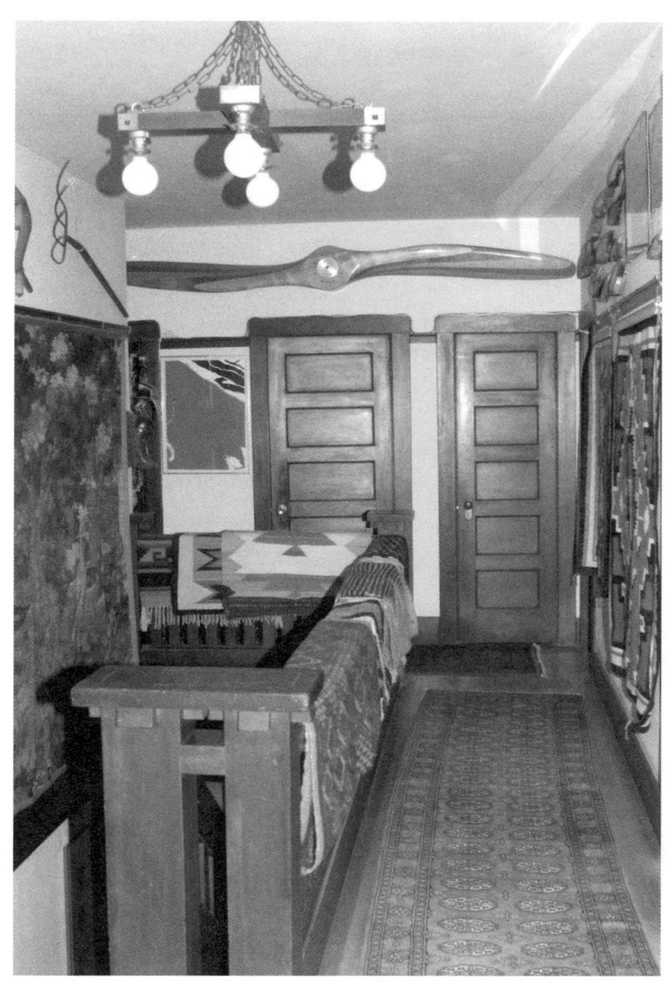

Upstairs hall joins bedrooms and studies. Ceiling light came from living room. Jim Adams made the wooden propeller.

Built-in storage at the end of hall is next to door to upstairs balcony.

original brick.

In 2001, the Adamses, defeated by a water-thirsty lawn that was too often ravaged by grub-seeking varmints, replanted with a mixture of drought-resistant perennials along the garden paths. These are bordered by used brick, much of it from the earthquake-damaged chimneys. The new design features a cottage garden at the front of the house, a hummingbird garden on the east side, and a cactus garden instead of the back lawn. ❋

SOURCES

Bassett, Lee Emerson. Appointment letter signed by David Starr Jordan, Stanford University (9 May 1900). Collection of Roberta Bassett Corson, Saratoga, California.

Bassett, Lee Emerson. Journals, 1900–1920 (especially 1909). Collection of Roberta Bassett Corson, Saratoga, California.

Bassett, Lee Emerson. Stanford University. Petition to Board of Trustees, Stanford University (30 November 1908). Stanford University Board of Trustees Supporting Documents, SC27, Box 1, Folder 10. Stanford University Archives.

Bassett, Lee Emerson. Letter to the Board of Trustees, Stanford University (30 November 1908). Collection of Roberta Bassett Corson, Saratoga, California.

Corson, Roberta Bassett. Interview with author, Stanford (1997).

"Hidden" Hadden Hill, a Mediterranean Gem [A. W. Smith], Fourth Annual Spring House Tour, Oakland Heritage Alliance (20 May 1990).

House plans, 740 Santa Ynez Street (1909). Collection of James and Marian Adams.

Memorial Resolution: Lee Emerson Bassett (1872–1959). Stanford University Academic Council.

Mitchell, J. Pearce, *Stanford University, 1916–41.* Stanford University Press (1958): 82, 86.

Nilan, Roxanne, "The English Club of Stanford University." *Sandstone & Tile* (Stanford Historical Society) 26, no. 1 (Winter/Spring 2002): 17.

The 1995 Annual Spring House Tour, Adams Point: Bellevue Avenue and Beyond [A. W. Smith], Oakland Heritage Alliance (25 May 1995).

The 1996 Annual Spring House Tour: The Historic 10th Avenue Historic District, nearby highlights of the Brooklyn Neighborhood [A. W. Smith], Oakland Heritage Alliance (19 May 1996).

Smith, A. W. "An Attractive Oakland Bungalow." *The Architect and Engineer* (August 1908).

Smith, A. W. Miscellaneous material provided by Betty Marvin, Planner I, Historical Preservation, Oakland Cultural Heritage Survey (1997), including "Historical Context: Unreinforced Masonry in Oakland, 1850–1948": 16.

Smith, A. W. "The Shingled House in California." *The Architect and Contractor of California* (20 May 1905).

Smith, Dr. Jay Ward. Interview with author, The Sequoias, Portola Valley, California (fall 1997).

"Speech by L. E. Bassett to the Western Speech Association, Thanksgiving Day 1947." Collection of Roberta Bassett Corson, Saratoga, California.

PHOTOS

Bassett, Bassett family; all others, Leni Hazlett.

747 Santa Ynez Street

(8 Aibonito, 8 Cabrillo, 747 Cabrillo)

BYRON FEIG

1909 ~ Tudor period style

ARCHITECT	OWNERS
John Bakewell Jr. of Bakewell and Brown	Hempl—Langnecker —Walker—Swain/Holmes

By Philip D. Leighton, David C. Weber, and Marian Leib Adams

In late 1906, taking advantage of Board of Trustees' concerns that faculty were choosing to live off campus, 12 professors petitioned for building sites around San Juan Hill. Professor George Hempl signed up for lot 5, nearly an acre on Aibonito Street (later renamed Cabrillo Street by President Jordan, then Santa Ynez).

The contractor was MacMackin. Construction, which began in early May 1909, went very fast, and on July 30 Hempl spent his first night in his new home.

The wood-framed house with gabled roof resembles a variation of a Tudor half-timber structure. However, instead of traditional wattle-and-daub filling in between the exposed timbers, it has stucco over fir framing.

It is a large house, with 14 rooms and three sunporches on two floors for a total of 4,282 square feet. The interior has a solid feel of comfort—this is a house designed for a family and for entertaining. It also has a full attic reached by a flight of stairs. The basement is a combination of crawl space and space of sufficient height to provide storage for family accumulations.

The layout of the two floors is essentially symmetrical around a great hall and staircase. On the entry level, the living room and library (now a billiard room) with their original oak floors are to the right, while the dining room, kitchen, laundry room, and breakfast porch are on the left. The second floor has four bedrooms along with three now-enclosed sleeping porches (one converted to a study, another to an exercise room). The house's four fireplaces are all functional.

On the second floor at the back of the staircase is one of the more interesting design features: a glazed passageway between two bedrooms at the back of the house; it may have been designed to display house plants. This 3- by 10-foot area has exterior and interior windows, and the floor is designed to shed water. Even without house plants, the two layers of glass forming the passageway are a visually interesting means of introducing natural light into the stair area.

The Owners

~George Hempl~

Hempl, a highly respected German philologist, was born at Whitewater, Wisconsin, in 1859. After graduating from the University of Michigan, he was a schoolteacher and then instructor in German at Johns Hopkins University. Three years of overseas study followed, and he received a Ph.D. from the university in Jena, Germany. He returned to Michigan in 1889, and from there was recruited by President David Starr Jordan.

Hempl arrived at Stanford in 1906 with his wife, Belle (Anna Belle Purmont), and two daughters. The Hempls first rented at 20 Lasuen Street on campus and then at 382 Lincoln Avenue in Palo Alto, but they needed to vacate that house by the end of 1908.

That spring, Hempl negotiated a lease on the property, but delays in financing the house's construction held up building for months. Finally, on September 11, 1908, the Board of Trustees approved a loan to Hempl of "about $7,000" at an interest rate of 6 percent. This was to be a grand house, greatly exceeding the minimum cost of $4,000 imposed by Jane Stanford in 1899. Not until April 1909 was

House façade today is unchanged from its appearance when it was built, in 1909. Intervening overgrowth has been removed and garden replanted.

George Hempl

the lease signed, a document that Hempl said he "had to sign...in an unsatisfactory way or have it delayed still longer." He attributed the delay to lawyers and business officers, noting that Jane Stanford's brother "Charles Lathrop was pleasant thru it all and evidently ment [sic] no harm. But his head is so made that he has to work in a mechanical way, dealing with only one thing at a time."

Construction had its ups and downs, and is well documented in Hempl's letters to his wife, who had returned to Ann Arbor. He wrote of his need to review and correct work every day, of his great satisfaction with the contractor, of the rapid progress, of the inadequate or inaccurate plans, and of the ideal location on the lot with sunshine in rooms at the best time of day. By the end of May, the house was up to the second story, a level that Hempl said was 1 foot higher than registrar Orrin Leslie Elliott's second floor (756 Santa Ynez) and level with the top of the dome of the library (Building 160 on the Quad). Nearby, Professor Arthur Clark's house (618 Mirada) was almost done. "Every one thinks the house is very large & it does look so," Hempl wrote of his house.

Although he economized in some ways (eliminating plaster on attic walls and painting of upstairs bedrooms, and some electrical fixtures), Hempl visited Steiger Terra Cotta and Pottery Works in San Francisco to select bricks for the fireplaces. He chose clinker bricks for his study, and elsewhere used both fine red bricks and others in cream or similar light colors, some having small specks of dark gray or black scattered through them, "which give them more character."

One day, Hempl discovered that it was too late to install an ash trap for the fireplace in his bedroom, so he talked the bricklayer, McClatchie, into installing an extra thickness between most of the furnace flue and the fireplace flues. Despite the inadequate plans and the details he had to catch or resolve almost daily, Professor Hempl wrote his wife frequently that "these are all trifles. I keep thinking how happy you will be there."

Decorated for a 2004 holiday house tour, white-painted staircase has interesting newel post carved to look like coiled rope.

Balusters on stairway and upstairs hall also have elaborate carving.

In early August, Hempl's daughter Hilda wrote that "work has begun on the electric line out here." She also raved about the house, adding that "we have arranged to get 2 qts of Jersey milk per day from Clarks. They got their cow yesterday.... They're going to have 2 acres of pasture down the hill, beyond Elliotts. Maybe we'll do the same."

~Renters Take Over~

When the Hempls returned to the University of Michigan during 1914–15, they rented the house to an attorney, Burrell G. White, and his wife, Alice Murton, a nurse; Miss M. Frisch, a governess, also lived there. As well, the Palo Alto city directory listed Ella H. Arnold, perhaps a cook or maid.

Returning to Stanford in 1915, the Hempls moved to Palo Alto—first at 609 Kingsley Avenue and then at 355 Kellogg Street. Possibly Professor Hempl's health forced the family into single-story houses. The Whites, along with Mrs. Arnold, stayed in the campus house until 1919. Mrs. Arnold remained, while San Francisco businessman J. Henry Meyer and his two daughters lived here when he was building "Atalya" in the wedge of high ground between Alpine and Sand Hill Roads, now known as the Meyer Buck Estate. Alice Meyer Buck and her sister, Olga Meyer, made significant donations to the university, including the 1966 Meyer Library in memory of their father and, in 1979, the estate.

The Palo Alto directory does not list renters for 1920–21, but Katherine Door, a maid, and Willard B. Pope, a civil engineer, and his wife, lived there.

Professor Hempl, having suffered from "slowly failing health," according to his memorial resolution, died in 1921. During 1924–25, the occupants were rancher William Wehner; his wife, Elizabeth; and Miss Ida. Also listed was Marie Colby, who served as cook.

In December 1924, Mrs. Hempl asked the Board of Trustees for an exception to the rule that campus houses could only be sold to qualified faculty and staff; she sought to sell the house to William Nichols of the New York Life Insurance Company. Her request was denied. From 1925 to 1927, the house was rented to Willard E. Hotchkiss, first dean of the Graduate School of Business, while his house on nearby El Escarpado Way was being constructed.

In 1928, during Herbert Hoover's campaign for the U.S. presidency, Hotchkiss moved out, and the house—about 100 yards from Hoover's house, on Mirada—was one of several converted for reporters.

The *Stanford Illustrated Review* in October 1928 reported that a campus committee made arrangements to lodge "the visiting correspondents in various fraternity houses and in Palo Alto. Press headquarters were established at the Phi Kappa Psi house [the old Cooksey House, 550 San Juan, now called Synergy], where both telegraph companies opened branch offices with elaborate equipment for handling correspondence."

While 747 Santa Ynez is not specifically mentioned in the *Review*, Edgar McDowell, class of 1926, remembered reporters being there. His family had built the house next door, at 739, where they lived until 1919, and his father,

Before and after: In the renovated living room (right), cream-colored walls with white trim cover Philippine mahogany paneling (left). It was installed in the 1950s over gray paint from wartime ROTC occupancy.

John Ezra McDowell, academic secretary and alumni secretary, was on the committee that made press arrangements.

Numerous extra telephone lines were installed throughout the house, connecting to an oversized junction box in the basement. For many years, that box also served several neighboring houses, a minor nuisance not removed until future owner Robert Walker had been in the house at least 15 years.

~Harry Leslie Langnecker~

The house was eventually sold (probably in 1929) to Dr. Langnecker, an orthopedic surgeon and associate professor at the Medical School. He was born in 1877 in New Brighton, Pennsylvania, and earned his A.B. in philosophy from Stanford in 1901 and M.D. from Johns Hopkins in 1906. After several years specializing in orthopedic surgery, he returned to Stanford in 1915. In 1914, he had married Joan Roome Macdonald, who died in 1927; they had two daughters, Leslie and Jane.

He lived at 747 with his daughters from 1929 until his death, in 1936. Medical professors Dr. George Barnett (living on Mirada) and Dr. Russel Lee (on Gerona), and their wives, took over legal guardianship of the Langnecker daughters. Leslie Langnecker Luttgens remembers the construction of the garage with two rental units above, and that Medical School students were among those renting the apartments. She also recalls that some mosaic fragments from the 1906 destruction of Memorial Church were found when the garage foundation was laid. Her father enclosed the first-floor porch on the north side with swing-out windows.

Elegant dining room also belies its past of gray wartime paint and Philippine mahogany.

In a list prepared in early 1939 of campus houses for sale, the "Estate of Dr. Langnecker" was given as the owner of 747 Santa Ynez. Most houses on the list had asking prices of $10,500 to $22,000; the Langnecker house is listed as "price not set." Any details from records of transfers of ownership and other university real estate records for the 1930s and 1940s were destroyed in the 1972 Encina fire.

At some point (no records available), the university bought the house and acted as landlord. In November 1939, a list of campus properties establishes Mrs. Mabel Wilber as a tenant of the Langnecker estate. In 1940 Margaret Lindsay, instructor in physiology, lived there for one quarter. It is not clear who lived there during 1937–39 and 1941–44. The house may have stood empty for some of the time.

During winter quarter 1944, the Navy ROTC Civil Affairs unit rented the house from Stanford. During this brief interval, it was called Wilson Hall, after Woodrow Wilson. (Other houses and fraternities used by the military in this era were named for presidents, including Roosevelt Hall and Taft Hall.) For the ROTC occupancy, four showers were installed in the basement, an arrangement that still exists.

In June 1944, Dr. Thomas LaCoste Schulte, a clinical instructor in surgery at the Medical School, expressed interest in renting the house. Citing this interest, Stanford's assistant business manager, E. S. Erwin, wrote to President Donald Tresidder: "This house is a white elephant, and if we could sell it at some reasonable price to one who is able to pay for it, it would be very desirable."

Tresidder responded:

> In answer to your inquiry about Dr. Schulte, it would appear that the wisest policy would be to adhere strictly to the principle of granting campus housing privileges only to full time faculty members who appear to be permanent and to such other members of the administrative staff whose position and length of service gives every indication of permanence. Accordingly, as a Clinical Instructor would not fall in the above definition, I consider that Dr. Schulte is not eligible for this privilege. In passing, I might say that I am entirely sympathetic with your problem in connection with this house and I hope that other possibilities will present themselves that will enable you to dispose of it.

English Professor James Aiken Work and his family rented from fall 1944 until September 1949, when they moved to 562 Foothill Boulevard. Work was a scholar of Chaucer and Laurence Sterne. During those years, three bedrooms in the house and an apartment over the garage were rented out.

~Robert A. Walker~

In August 1949, Robert Walker, professor of political science, bought the house from Stanford, and in September he and his wife, Louise, and their three sons moved in.

Walker was born in 1914 in Spokane, Washington. He received his undergraduate and doctoral degrees at the University of Chicago, and after positions in government taught political science at Kansas State University. At Stanford, he chaired the Political Science Department from 1958 to 1963.

President Sterling and Provost Terman soon recognized Walker's administrative abilities. On various committees, he helped to review and restructure the undergraduate curriculum for the first time in 40 years (1954), develop plans for Stanford Industrial Park and new faculty-staff housing areas on campus (late 1950s and 1960s), and create, with Professor Friedrich Strothmann, Department of German Studies, the overseas studies program (1958).

The Academic Council memorial resolution of April 1999 aptly summed up his contributions: "Bob Walker's boundless energy and spirit of public service left a lasting imprint on the development of Stanford. He was not only a skilled administrator, but also an innovator of great vision. He played a proud part in the improvement and growth of Stanford from his arrival in 1949 to his retirement in 1976."

When the Walkers moved in, the entire interior of the house was still painted Navy gray; the color remained until the mid-'50s, when the Walkers installed Philippine mahogany paneling over the original walls. It is speculated that the addition of the wood paneling contributed significantly to the relative lack of damage from the 1989 Loma Prieta earthquake (one fireplace and a few small windows were cracked, the front porch collapsed, and a large fish tank spilled in the living room).

Robert A. Walker

The Walkers also removed heavy growth of bougainvillea and wisteria that largely hid the exterior of the house. Leslie Langnecker Luttgens remembers the east side of the house being "quite a wilderness," with snakes and rather dense growth, and she believes there once was a tennis court on the property. This court may have been the badminton court used by the Walker family in the early years of their occupancy, but which is now grown over with trees and shrubs. In 1956, the backyard was redone with a design prepared by Victor King Thompson, professor of architecture at Stanford. Today this area boasts a delightful seating area and a two-level decorative pool of Thompson's design. A koi pond with lattice canopy, both designed by Professor Walker, is within sight of the sitting area. The upper back corner of the property has an enclosed dog run.

In the 1950s, the Walkers modernized the kitchen, removing the original Temple stove, which could burn wood or trash for supplemental heat. They added heat to the enclosed first-floor porch and turned it into a bright breakfast room. After refinishing the original hardwood floors, they installed wall-to-wall carpet throughout most of the house. The original knob-and-tube wiring was replaced over the years except for a few examples in the basement and attic.

By and large, the changes over the years have been modest. The Walkers did find some evidence of renovation work done perhaps in the 1930s, particularly in one bathroom.

Perhaps the greatest change is in the growth of the surrounding plantings. One of the Hempl daughters was quite interested in biology, and she is credited with planting many trees. An early photo was described as being largely vacant of plantings, and the house was described as standing out with considerable prominence. Today, this is hardly the case, as the shrubs and trees have grown to maturity. The original front gravel path still exists, though the main approach to the house today is by the driveway from the opposite front corner of the lot.

~Judith L. Swain and Edward Holmes~

After Robert Walker's death, in 1998, the house was sold to Dr. Swain, professor and chair of the Department of Medicine, and Dr. Holmes, a specialist in genetics and metabolic diseases and at the time senior associate dean for research at Stanford Medical School. In 1999, he left Stanford for Duke University but is now vice chancellor for Health Sciences and dean of the School of Medicine at the University of California, San Diego, so the couple commutes between Stanford and La Jolla on weekends. In the 2005–06 academic year, Dr. Swain will become dean for translational research and director of the College of Integrated Life Sciences at UCSD. In early spring 2005, the house was sold once again.

Swain received her B.S. in chemistry from UCLA in 1970 and M.D. from UCSD in 1974. After faculty positions at Duke University Medical Center and the University of Pennsylvania, she came to Stanford in 1996. Swain is widely known in the field of molecular cardiology, and pioneered the use of transgenic animals to understand the genetic basis of cardiovascular development and disease. Holmes, an international expert in the molecular basis of human disease, was born in Winona, Mississippi, and received his undergraduate degree from Washington and Lee University and his medical training at the University of Pennsylvania.

When Swain and Holmes bought the house, it was very dark, yet full of promise. They made no structural changes that would alter the architectural integrity of the original design. A wall overhanging the back patio was taken down, as was a windbreak fence between the back of the house and the garage. These changes opened up the patio and brought a lot of light into the south side of the house. The garage roof was replaced, and new doors were added. The downstairs fireplaces were converted to gas, the electrical system was modernized, and air-conditioning added. In addition, all windows on the south side of the house were replaced, the driveway was repaved, and the earthquake-damaged front porch was redone.

A major transformation came from a new coat of paint. To lighten the interior, the wood-paneled walls were painted cream. The wood trim is white, which reveals lovely detailing in the decorative and supporting beams. The dark wall-to-wall carpet downstairs was removed and the original oak floors restored.

Decorative painting of borders and patterns transformed the old linoleum floors in a sunporch and the kitchen, and was also used to lighten the kitchen cabinets. In the dining and living rooms, the walls have been glazed for an attractive and unique finish.

Bathrooms have been improved with new toilets and paint, but most of the colorful original tile remains.

When the garden was cleared out, it revealed a

Upstairs, a narrow passage—with small-paned windows facing back garden on one side, upstairs hall on the other—brings light farther into the house. Most likely, house plants grew in the glassed-in space.

number of paths winding around the house. Dr. Swain dug out the koi pond and restocked it. On stairs up to Mirada, near the Hoover House, remnants of pre-1906 earthquake Memorial Church were revealed. The front garden has been completely relandscaped, but the rest has been tamed, and most of the original plantings remain.

With its wide, spacious halls and rooms, the house seems to have been built for entertaining. Each year Dr. Swain invited the Department of Medicine office staff to a Christmas party for tree trimming. Staff members would bring presents that were then taken to Lucile Packard Children's Hospital. In the late summer, Department of Medicine interns and their families, and house staff were welcomed with margaritas and festivities on the patio and in the garden. ❋

Upstairs room gains light through glass-paned doors. Ceiling fixture is original.

SOURCES

Behrens, Earl. " 'Covering' the Hoover Party on Campus." *Stanford Illustrated Review* (October 1928): 17.

"Edward W. Holmes, M.D., Selected as New Vice Chancellor for Health Sciences" [news release]. *UCSD School of Medicine News* (20 July 2000).

Hempl, George. Lease and loan documents. Stanford Board of Trustees Supporting Documents, SC27, Stanford University Archives.

Hempl, George [obit]. *Daily Palo Alto Times* (15 Aug 1921).

Langneker, Harry L. [obit]. *Palo Alto Times* (24 September 1936).

Luttgens, Leslie Langnecker. Telephone interview with David Weber (1994).

McDowell, Edgar. Interview with Karen Bartholomew, Palo Alto (January 2004).

Memorial Resolution: George Hempl (d. 1921). Stanford University Academic Council.

Memorial Resolution: Harry Leslie Langnecker (d. 1936). Stanford University Academic Council.

Memorial Resolution: Robert Averill Walker (1914–1998). Stanford University Academic Council.

Peters, Scott. E-mail to Margaret McKinnon re his grandfather Harry L. Langnecker (April 2004).

Swain, Dr. Judith. Interview with Marian Adams, Stanford (April 2002).

Tresidder, Donald B. Presidential records, Stanford University Archives.

Walker, Robert. Interview with Philip Leighton and David Weber, Stanford (1994).

Wilbur, Ray Lyman. Presidential papers, SC64, Stanford University Archives.

Work, James. E-mails to Marian Adams re his parents' tenancy and other renters (July 2004, March 2005).

PHOTOS

Hempl, Stanford Archives; Walker, Stanford News Service; living room before, collection of Judith Swain; all others, Leni Hazlett.

755 Santa Ynez Street

(6 Cabrillo, 755 Cabrillo)

BYRON FEIG

1915 ~ Tudor period style, Craftsman details

ARCHITECT	OWNERS
John K. Branner	Fairclough—Williams—Cohen

BY JOHN HARBAUGH AND MARIAN LEIB ADAMS

Still imposing on its two-thirds-acre lot, this house was monarch of all it surveyed when it was built, in 1915. Views extended to all four points of the compass, and though mature trees block out the distance today, the house itself is little changed.

The house's size is impressive: about 3,700 square feet on two main floors. It was designed by John K. Branner, a son of Stanford's second president, John Casper Branner. The builder and building costs are unknown.

Branner, a masterful designer, utilized features of the Craftsman and Tudor styles to great advantage. The half-timber and stucco exterior walls above the first floor reflect Tudor influences, but a sharp eye will see Craftsman elements, too. The wide eaves with exposed rafters and projecting beams are prominent Craftsman details, as are the shingles for the exterior of the first floor and slight upward curve in the rooflines. The many gables are common to both Craftsman and Tudor styles. The exposed timbers project only slightly from the stucco. Interestingly, they run only vertically or horizontally, without any diagonal timbers commonly associated with Tudor houses.

The front of the house is strongly asymmetrical. Sheltering the west-facing front porch is an overhanging roof supported by 10-inch-square pillars, which flare outward at the top. The relatively gentle slope of the roofs —about 25°—is typical of the Craftsman style. (By contrast, Tudor-style roofs are typically steeper.)

Supporting the front roof are sturdy horizontal beams, which in turn support the rafters. Above and to the left of the entry porch, a prominent bay window with angled sides cantilevers out from the house, supported by curving brackets. On the house's right side, another gabled projection has large triangular brackets for support. Centered below the projection is a prominent floor-to-ceiling bay with two large windows on the front, and slightly narrower windows on the two angled sides.

The back of the house features a flat-roofed sunroom with double doors to the back garden. In the original plans, the porch's roof had a railing or balustrade, though, paradoxically, no access door to the roof.

Most notable on the rear side is a 14-foot-wide two-story wing projecting 20 feet beyond the main part of the house. The wing's second floor, originally a screened porch, was glassed in by the present owners. The lower floor, including a single-story wing that projects 12 feet farther, contains part of the kitchen and breakfast room, a bedroom, and a bath. (The original configuration for the back of the house included a service porch with laundry tub and washer, a maid's room, and bathroom.)

Drawings of front (west, above) and side (south, right) show the richness of Craftsman-style details: vertical timbers, small-paned windows, bay windows, porch pillars.

ELENA ANGOLOTI

The 8-foot-tall front door has multipaned windows on each side. It opens to a 12-foot-square entry hall, still lit by two original copper chandeliers. An 18th-century grandfather clock emphasizes the predominantly English feel of the house's interior.

Wood paneling, wainscoting, and beamed ceilings dominate the interior; all are old-growth redwood, as is the front door. Treatment with tung oil maintains the wood. The golden oak floors in the hallways and principal downstairs rooms are original.

The interior's most notable feature is the 14- by 24-foot living room to the right of the entry hall; ceiling beams run across its width. An immense fireplace dominates the room, its massive blocks of sandstone perhaps from campus buildings that collapsed during the 1906 earthquake. Wainscoting has grooves along its top for displaying china plates. A built-in seat in the bay window has been removed, but original wall light fixtures remain.

Across the entry hall, the dining room has west-facing windows overlooking the front garden, and a bay window on the north side. The right-hand wall's built-in sideboard has slender china cabinets with leaded-glass doors on each side. The chandelier and light fixtures are original. To the left of the sideboard is a door to the spacious and much modified kitchen. Originally, this wall had two doors: a swinging door to a butler's pantry (with another swinging door from there into the kitchen) and another door into a narrow back hall with stairs to the basement.

In the late 1950s, the second owners reconfigured the kitchen, butler's pantry, service porch, and maid's quarters. The pantry and back hall became the family kitchen, and the original kitchen became part of an apartment for elderly parents, with the maid's quarters as their bedroom suite.

In this photo from 1958, plantings crowd the house, hiding its details.

Behind the entry hall is the stairway hall; in each corner is a square redwood column with fluted sides. French doors lead to a redwood deck overlooking the back garden. Newel posts on the curved stairway to the second floor repeat the columns' design on a smaller scale. Four-foot-high redwood wainscoting lines the stair wall.

Across from the staircase are a small bathroom and a redwood-paneled study. The study's handsome redwood fireplace still has its original blue-and-green ceramic tile surround and hearth; below a small bay window are a built-in bench and wood storage. The sunroom off the bookshelf-lined study is temporarily being used for storage.

Upstairs are five bedrooms, two of which have been enlarged by enclosing former sleeping porches. The feeling here is lighter, with more white-painted plaster and less redwood paneling. The floors are fir, and the window and closet door framing is redwood. There are two baths, one off the master bedroom that is shared with a smaller bedroom or sewing room, and one in the hall, with the original separation of bath and water closet.

An attic over the main part of the house is reached by a stairway. The interior height along the ridgeline is about 7 feet. Though the sloping roof restricts headroom, the space is usable and well lit by dormers on the front and rear of the house, and by low windows on the sides. In the partial basement, small windows on the house's rear side bring in daylight.

Many of the original plantings that existed when the second owners bought the house still exist today, including the redwood tree at the center of the backyard, and pepper and birch trees in front. But an enormous oak tree that shaded the front walk and a eucalyptus that towered over the back yard have succumbed. The present owners added a redwood deck and a detached garage at the back of the house; their children used the garage as a studio for playing rock music.

The Owners

~Henry Rushton Fairclough~

Fairclough was born in Barrie, Ontario, in 1862 and received his B.A. and M.A. from the University of Toronto in 1883 and 1886, respectively; in 1922, Toronto also conferred on him an honorary doctorate of letters. After study at Johns Hopkins University in Baltimore, Fairclough arrived at Stanford in the fall of 1893, as associate professor of Latin and Greek. Two years later, he returned to Johns Hopkins to complete his Ph.D., which he received in 1896. Back at Stanford, he was promoted to full professor with three titles: professor of Greek, professor of Latin, and professor of classical philology.

When he became emeritus, in 1927, he was professor of Latin and chairman of the department. His memorial resolution noted:

> Professor Fairclough spent forty years of glorious teaching and research...he found time, somewhere and somehow, to contribute 135 books, texts, translations, articles, reviews and addresses to the literature of his profession... his translations of Horace and Vergil will be classics for years and years to come;... His vigor was tireless and a despair to colleagues and friends trailing with him over hills and vales.

With his wife, Frederica, and daughter, Katrine, Professor Fairclough lived initially on Salvatierra Street and later on Alvarado Row. Opting for a larger house, in 1914 the family decided to build on San Juan Hill. The degree to which they provided instructions to architect John K. Branner is unknown, although Fairclough states in his autobiography, *Warming Both Hands,* that in the summer of 1914 his wife and daughter were making plans for the new house they hoped to build shortly "upon the hill," while he was busy with his books and classes. From this we may assume that Mrs. Fairclough probably had a substantial role in providing instructions to Branner; perhaps Katrine, then aged 25, did as well.

Fairclough wrote:

> We were among the first to secure a desirable site, commanding a very fine view. Many a day we strolled up to the summit, looked down upon the peaceful waters of Lagunita Lake [sic] and the red-tiled roofs of the Quad, and then drank our fill of the more distant prospect, Mount Tamalpais to the north, Mount Diablo and Mount Hamilton to the east, Loma Prieta and the Santa Cruz heights to the south, and, near by, the sable Black Mountain range to the west.

Henry Rushton Fairclough

In 1910, Katrine entered Stanford. Earlier, her mother's nephew and Katrine's cousin, James Fergusson, had stayed with the family when he was an undergraduate at Stanford. The Faircloughs had "come to love him as a son." After graduating in 1908, James attended medical school at Johns Hopkins University in Baltimore, obtaining an M.D. degree with distinction in 1914.

Meanwhile, Katrine had graduated with Phi Beta Kappa honors from Stanford in June 1914. Like her cousin, she decided to study medicine at Johns Hopkins. However, her health failed, and she returned home to train in physical therapy at the University of California Medical School, in San Francisco.

When World War I broke out, James was commissioned in the Royal Army Medical Corps and assigned to the military hospital at Southampton, England. In October 1915, he was transferred to the Eighth Battalion of the Black Watch and sent to France.

Katrine corresponded with him, describing details of the house while it was under construction in 1915. In one of his replies, he wrote: "Well, I'd like to see your new house. Once you've got used to it, I know it will be a pride and pleasure. How well I remember the other! It's a funny thing—in a life like this, when you're never sure when your

Large living room has sandstone-block fireplace and massive beams across the ceiling.

turn will come, memories and interests, instead of being dulled and obliterated by your own concern for yourself, become more vivid than real."

Then he asked about John Branner the architect, about many of his Stanford friends, as well as other students and faculty. James was killed in action in 1916 while leading an attack on the German position at the village of Longueval, in the Somme.

In the spring of 1917, Katrine Fairclough and her close friend Margaret Stevenson volunteered for orthopedic rehabilitation work with the British armed forces. They sailed to England and, after passing examinations, were admitted to Lady Paget's Corps of Nurses and sent to Liverpool, where they cared for wounded soldiers at Alder Hey Orthopaedic Hospital.

Fairclough relates that "when Katrine sailed for England, she had no suspicion that her father was to go overseas also. But I was very anxious to 'do my bit,' and although too old for military service I hoped to find some worth-while job in a civilian capacity." A short time later, he was asked to serve with the newly formed Commission of the Red Cross, which would attend primarily to the needs of American prisoners of war. At the end of spring semester 1917, he traveled to England, coincidentally on the same Cunard liner, *Orduna,* that had taken Katrine and her friend to England three months earlier. From England, he traveled to Paris to make arrangements at the American Embassy to travel to Red Cross headquarters in Bern, Switzerland.

Fairclough remained in Bern until the spring of 1919, after which he expected to return to California. However, the commissioner of the Red Cross asked him to serve with its newly organized Commission of the Balkan States. Given the tumult in the Balkans, it was deemed necessary that he be commissioned as an officer in the U.S. Army, and was immediately appointed as a captain. Upon arrival in Rome, he was promoted to major and learned that his destination would be Montenegro.

After a year in Montenegro, Fairclough returned home in the summer of 1920. He wrote:

> My happy return to home and family and academic halls was a happy event. I felt as if I had laid aside a mountain of care and responsibility.... Stanford was a peaceful retreat, where life ran very smoothly, and here at least those of us who from time to time strayed away in foreign parts could appreciate the good fortune of the dwellers among the *arva, beata arva* [Horace: "fields, blessed fields"] of the Stanford Farm. Our family was reunited. My wife had managed nobly in the absence of both husband and daughter, and both house and grounds showed the happy results of her careful supervision.

Subsequent events at the Fairclough house, however, proved to be mixed. Katrine married Rufus Kimball, and a daughter, Margaret, was born in December 1926. The joy of the new grandchild's arrival was soon tempered because Mrs. Fairclough died just a month later. (Three years later, Fairclough married Mary Charlotte Holly in Paris.)

During these years, his granddaughter was among the lights of his life. Unfortunately, she had serious health problems and had to be sent to special schools as her health declined. She died at the age of 9. Though he had retired at the mandatory age of 65, he remained active as a scholar and lived in the house until his death, in 1938.

Bay window in living room faces front garden.

From the back of the entry hall, redwood stairway heads to second floor. Note wainscoting up the stairs, and carved detail on pillars.

~HARRY WILLIAMS~

The second owners bought the house in 1943 for $10,000 and lived there until 1966, raising two children. Williams, a professor of civil engineering, was born in 1901 in Nevada but spent most of his adult life in the Santa Clara Valley. After a year at College of the Pacific (then in San Jose), he transferred to Stanford, graduating in civil engineering in 1925. He worked for Standard Oil Company for five years, then returned to Stanford, where he received the degree of Engineer in 1933 and joined the faculty of the Department of Civil Engineering. His professional career focused on the effects of earthquakes on structures, fatigue resistance of various materials, and port and coastal engineering. After he retired in 1966, he taught at the University of Hawaii for two years. He died in 1982.

Gertrude Smoyer Williams was a force in her own right. She earned a degree in English and economics from UC Berkeley, then worked as a copywriter for an advertising agency in San Francisco. After her marriage, in 1929, she continued to work to support her husband's schooling. Later, she was active in the League of Women Voters, American Friends Service Committee, and Peninsula School in Menlo Park. She was also a co-founder of the Palo Alto Co-op and an adviser to foreign students at Stanford. She died in 1997.

~PAUL COHEN~

Paul and Christina Cohen have occupied the house since 1966, raising their three sons there. All of them attended Stanford.

From 1950 to 1953, Paul Cohen was a student at Brooklyn College. He received both his master's and doctoral degrees at the University of Chicago, in 1954 and 1958, respectively. He spent 1957–58 as an instructor at the University of Rochester, 1958–59 at M.I.T., and 1959–61 as a fellow at the Institute for Advanced Study at Princeton.

Cohen came to Stanford in 1961 and was promoted to professor of mathematics in 1964. His earlier research included work on partial differential equations and harmonic analysis. Among his awards are the Bôcher Memorial Prize from the American Mathematical Society in 1964, the Fields Medal at the International Congress of Mathematicians in Moscow in 1966 for his fundamental work on the foundations of set theory, and the National Medal of Science in 1967. He is a member of the National Academy of Sciences.

Cohen has the distinction of solving one of the 23 fundamental problems the German mathematician David Hilbert included in a speech delivered to the Second International Congress of Mathematicians in Paris in 1900. to find solutions, and some remain unsolved. ❋

In 1948, Williams parents and children posed in the living room (above). A few years earlier, Brian and Susan read a story on the fireplace hearth.

Redwood bracket on study fireplace has an ornate carved design.

Small-paned windows and French doors bring in eastern light to the stair hall. Ceiling light fixtures are original.

SOURCES

Biographical file [Paul Cohen]. Stanford University Archives.

Biographical file [Harry Williams]. Stanford University Archives.

"Earthquake Expert Harry Williams Died on Christmas Day." *Campus Report* (5 January 1983): 7.

Fairclough, Henry Rushton, *Warming Both Hands: The Autobiography of Henry Rushton Fairclough*. Stanford University Press (1941).

"Gertrude Williams" [obit]. *Stanford Report* (21 May 1997).

Harwood, Lee, and Lee Ziegler. Conversations about Gertrude Williams with Marian Leib Adams (2004).

"Harry A. Williams, 1901–1982" [news release]. Stanford News Service (29 December 1982).

"Harry Williams, Emeritus Professor" [obit]. *Peninsula Times Tribune* (29 December 1982): B-6.

House plans and renovation plans. Stanford University Maps and Records.

House renovation details. Stanford University Faculty Housing records.

Kato, Donna. "A League of Their Own" [Gertrude Williams]. *San Jose Mercury News* (19 May 1995): 1H, 3H.

Lundstrom, Mack. "Gertrude Williams, Political Activist" [obit]. *San Jose Mercury News* (31 May 1997): 6B.

Memorial resolution: Harry A. Williams (1901–1982). Stanford University Academic Council.

Memorial resolution: Henry Rushton Fairclough (1862–1938). Stanford University Academic Council.

"Paul J. Cohen awarded the Fields Medal." Stanford News Service (16 August 1966).

Turner, Paul V., Wattis Professor of Art. Exterior house tour with John Harbaugh (2003).

Williams, Brian K. Interview with Marian Leib Adams (28 August 2004).

PHOTOS

1958 exterior and Williams photos, Williams family collection; Fairclough, Stanford Archives; all others, Leni Hazlett.

MISCELLANEOUS REFERENCES

American Men and Women of Science, 12th ed. New York: Bowker (1971).

Death indexes

California Death Index. California Department of Health Services Office of Health Information and Research: Vital Statistics Section. www.vitalsearchca.com/gen/ca_vitals/cadeathm.htm

Palo Alto obituaries on line: http://www.cityofpaloalto.org/library/reference/resourcesonline.html

Social Security Death Index: http://ssdi.rootsweb.com/

Endowed professorships & directorships at Stanford University. Stanford, California: Board of Trustees of Stanford University (2000).

Fire insurance map of Palo Alto, Calif., for the exclusive use of agents in Palo Alto, Calif. San Francisco: Sanborn (1908).

Fire insurance maps of 1924, and a later sheet with multiple overlays to update field conditions. San Francisco: Sanborn (1924).

Gebhard, David, Eric Sandweiss, and Robert Winter. *The Guide to Architecture in San Francisco and Northern California.* Rev. ed. New York: Peregrine Smith Books, (1985).

House specifications. Office of Plant Services Records, SC 123, Box 4B, Stanford University Archives.

Joncas, Richard, David J. Neumann, and Paul V. Turner. *The Campus Guide: Stanford Campus.* New York: Princeton Architectural Press (1999).

Guggenheim fellowship information: http://www.gf.org/25fellow.html

McAlester, Virginia, and Lee McAlester. *A Field Guide to American Houses.* New York: Alfred A. Knopf, Inc. (2003).

Palo Alto and environs city directories (1895/96–1978).

Palo Alto v. 1 (monthly, 1891–92). Stanford, California.

Palo Alto Times [variously called *Daily Palo Alto Times* and *Peninsula Times Tribune*]. (5 January 1893–8 September 1984). Palo Alto, California.

Stanford Daily v. 1– (9 September 1892–) [called *The Daily Palo Alto* (9 September 1892–20 August 1926)]. Stanford, California.

Stanford News Service: http://www.stanford.edu/dept/news/html/

Stanford Quad v. 1– (1894–). Stanford, California.

Stanford University Academic Council. Memorial resolutions: http://histsoc.stanford.edu

Stanford University Alumni Directory. Stanford (1910, 1931, 1955, 1984).

Stanford University directories

List of officers and students. Stanford (1891–94).

Annual register. Stanford (1891/92–1946/47).

Directory of officers and students. Stanford (1932/33–1947/48).

University directory. Stanford (1947/48–1961/62).

Faculty/staff directory. Stanford (1962/63–1989/90).

Stanford directory. Stanford: Stanford Student Enterprizes (1991–).

Who's Who in America v. 1 (1899–1900). Chicago: Marquis (1899–).

Who's Who of American Women and Women of Canada, 4th ed. Chicago: A. N. Marquis Co. (1966–67).

Who Was Who in America (1607–1896). Chicago: Marquis Who's Who (1963).